**Architectural Design** 56 1/2-1986

Editorial Offices: 42 Leinster Gardens, London W2 Telephone: 01-40[...] [...]d Street London W8

EDITOR
**Dr Andreas C Papa[...]**
HOUSE EDITOR: Frank [...]
CONSULTANTS: Catherine Cooke, Dennis Crompton, Terry Farrell,
Kenneth Frampton, Charles Jencks, Leon Krier, Robert Maxwell, Demetri Porphyrios, Colin Rowe, Derek Walker

## Architectural Design Profile 63

# THE NATIONAL GALLERY

Campbell Zogolovitch Wilkinson & Gough.

In February of this year the National Gallery in London announced Robert Venturi of Venturi, Rauch and Scott Brown as the architect of the new Hampton Site Extension to house one of the world's finest collections of Early Renaissance art. This marked the culmination of a train of events started some years ago with an open competition and ending in public outrage and scandal.

Following the Sainsbury brothers' generous donation which removed the previous requirement to have commercial office space incorporated within the building, a total of six architects were shortlisted to submit reports so that the Board of Trustees could select not a winning scheme but an architect with whom they could work successfully towards the final design of the building. This *Architectural Design* Profile, which is intended as an interim report between the discussions in recent issues and publication of the eventual scheme in about a year's time, presents the designs of the five unsuccessful practices, much in the manner of a Salon des Refusés. Each scheme is described in the architect's own words, and is illustrated with plans, elevations and perspective drawings as well as models showing the extension *in situ*.

TYPICAL GALLERY DETAILS                                    1:10

Colquhoun + Miller with RMJM.

# A.D. Architectural Design Profile

# THE NATIONAL GALLERY

Campbell Zogolovitch Wilkinson & Gough.

CAMPBELL, ZOGOLOVITCH WILKINSON & GOUGH

Campbell Zogolovitch Wilkinson & Gough, perspective view from Trafalgar Square.

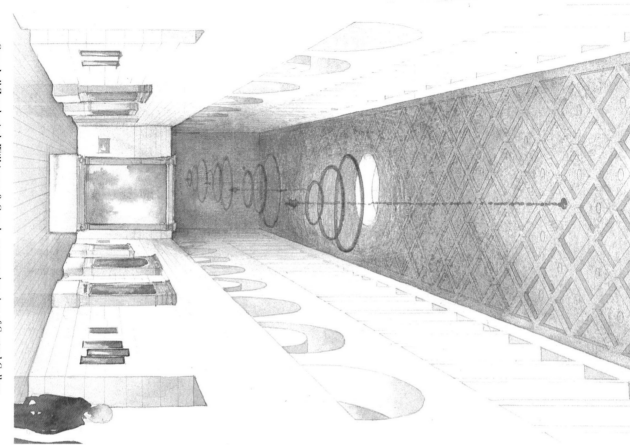

Campbell Zogolovitch Wilkinson & Gough, perspective view of Central Gallery.

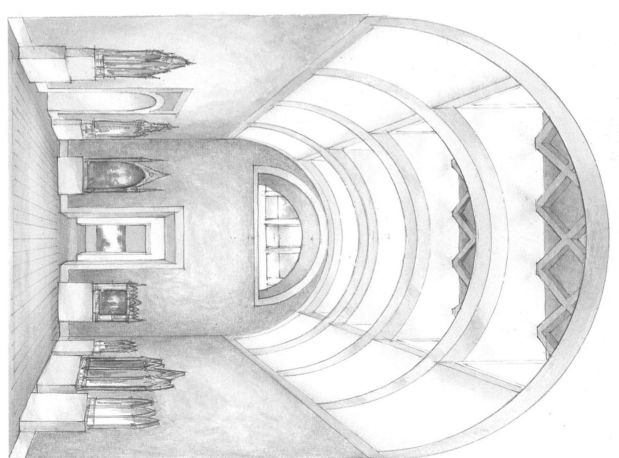

Campbell Zogolovitch Wilkinson & Gough, perspective view of Gallery 2.

**CAMPBELL ZOGOLOVITCH WILKINSON & GOUGH**

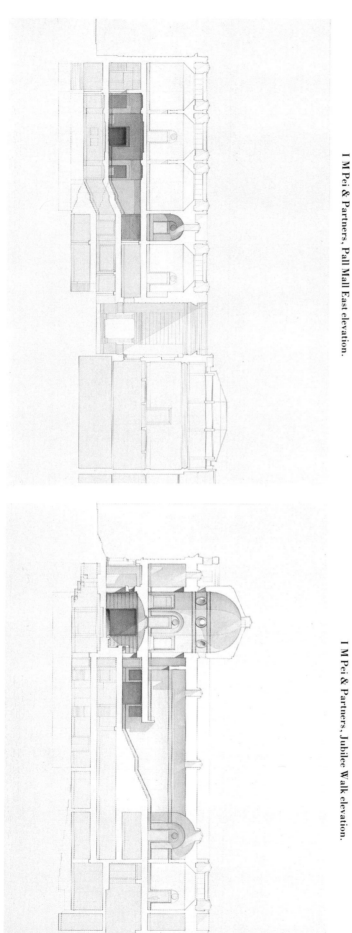

I M Pei & Partners, section looking north.

I M Pei & Partners, section looking west.

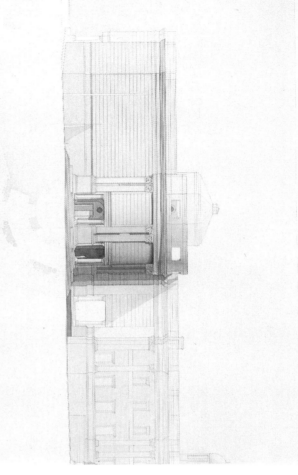

I M Pei & Partners, Pall Mall East elevation.

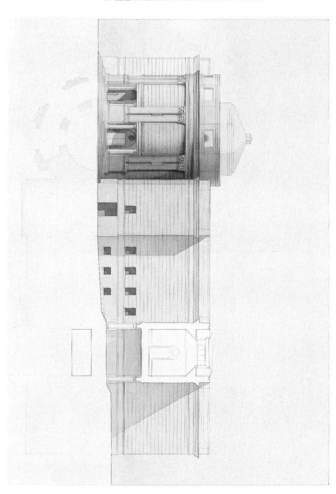

I M Pei & Partners, Jubilee Walk elevation.

HENRY N COBB OF I M PEI & PARTNERS

I M Pei & Partners, elevation detail.

HENRY N COBB OF I M PEI & PARTNERS

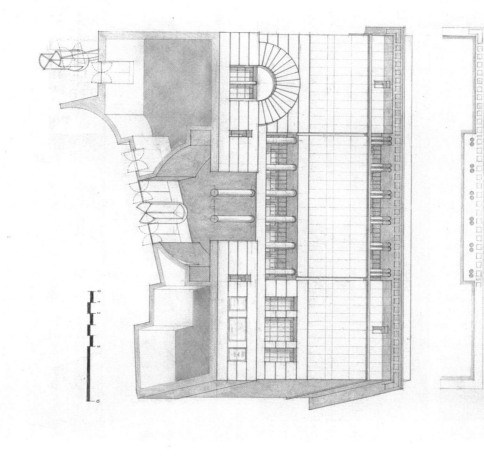

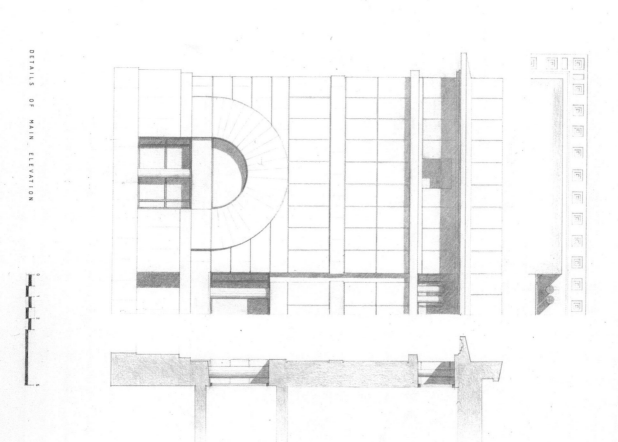

COLQUHOUN + MILLER WITH RMJM

PROJECTED MAIN ELEVATION

Colquhoun + Miller with RMJM, projected main elevation.

DETAILS OF MAIN ELEVATION

Colquhoun + Miller with RMJM, details of main elevation.

# THE NATIONAL GALLERY

## PROJECTS BY

Jeremy Dixon & BDP
Campbell Zogolovitch Wilkinson & Gough
Henry N Cobb of I M Pei & Partners
Colquhoun + Miller with RMJM
James Stirling Michael Wilford & Associates

# Jeremy Dixon and BDP

## Introduction

The National Gallery's new building must be a distinguished addition to the present Gallery and to Trafalgar Square, and should house, in a worthy manner, the unique Early Renaissance Collection.

The Gallery is seeking, at this stage, an architect, and not necessarily a building. It has been emphasised to competitors that the design should be an initial proposal demonstrating an architectural approach, rather than a definitive scheme. This approach should identify accurately the most important issues and aspects of the project while leaving open the opportunity for future development with the Gallery staff.

The 'Design Approach' section of this presentation has been divided into two parts – the building looked at in terms of Trafalgar Square, and the building looked at in terms of the paintings – to reflect our view that there are two primary issues to be addressed. In the first part, we look in detail at the site and its setting and discuss a possible organisation of the issue rather than being taken as a definitive solution. This section also expresses an attitude to the quality of the new building as a self-contained entity rather than primarily an 'extension'. In the second part, the discussion starts with the paintings and looks at how the gallery layout might be derived from an understanding of the collection and the way the paintings might be played.

The lighting of galleries is one of the more difficult and contentious aspects of the project. In this section we discuss a proposal that is intended to provoke discussion of the issue rather than being taken as a definitive solution. This section also expresses an attitude to the quality of

It is difficult to avoid arriving at a building proposal, because the issues can only be made clear to ourselves and the National Gallery in the context of a specific solution. The section on 'The Building' deals with all the accommodation in the brief in plan and section.

The external appearance of the building is primarily sensitive in relation to Trafalgar Square and its approaches. The section on 'Perspectives' takes the studies of the external appearance of the building and tests them at eye-level from the various viewpoints around the Square. Photographs of the model from similar viewpoints are included in parallel.

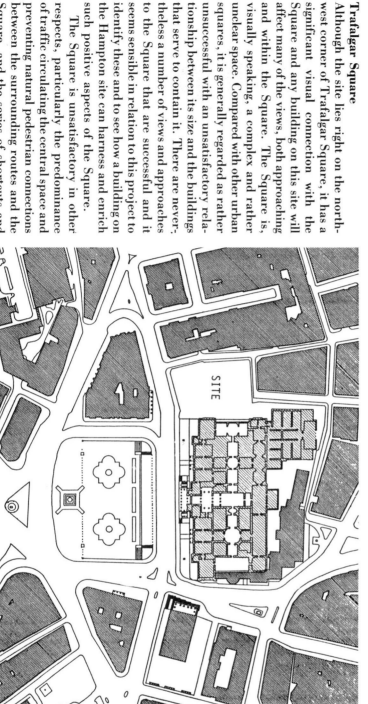

SITE

Site plan.

## Trafalgar Square

Although the site lies right on the north-west corner of Trafalgar Square, it has a significant visual connection with the Square and any building on this site will affect many of the views, both approaching and within the Square. The Square is, visually speaking, a complex and rather unclear space. Compared with other urban squares, it is generally regarded as rather unsuccessful with an unsatisfactory relationship between its size and the buildings that serve to contain it. There are nevertheless a number of views and approaches to the Square that are successful and it seems sensible in relation to this project to identify these and to see how a building on the Hampton site can harness and enrich such positive aspects of the Square.

The Square is unsatisfactory in other respects, particularly the predominance of traffic circulating the central space and preventing natural pedestrian connections between the surrounding routes and the Square, and the series of shortcuts and diagonal routes. However, there is a limit to what can be solved when considering one small portion of the Square that is itself almost on the fringes of the main

the change in level from the pavement outside the Gallery to the Square could be exploited as a pedestrian underpass. Perhaps, even, traffic should be diverted away from the north side of the Square altogether. These all seem valid long-term possibilities when considering the use of the Square as a whole, but have little immediate effect on the development of a scheme for the Hampton site itself.

Two of the most successful visual progressions in relation to Trafalgar Square are the approaches along the north side, on the one hand from Charing Cross and on the other down Pall Mall. Both of these sequences involve the Hampton site and the entry to the existing Gallery. The one from Charing Cross has the additional significance of being the forecourt to a main-line station. Most visitors to the Square and the Gallery probably arrive along the north edge from Pall Mall/Piccadilly, Leicester Square, St Martin's Lane and Charing Cross. An exception to this is the location of the exits from Trafalgar Square tube station. Less important in terms of the number of people approaching the Square, but significant in formal terms, is the relationship of

Whitehall to the Square and to the axis of the existing Gallery. The next section of this report takes the three approaches — Charing Cross, Pall Mall and Whitehall — and examines them in greater detail in relation to the Hampton site.

The map is drawn to emphasise the public spaces and to identify the location of the Hampton site. The Gallery building is hatched, while the primary structure of galleries is left white to emphasise the formal connection between the main entrance to the existing Gallery and the point of connection to an extension on the Hampton site.

area. Perhaps the pavements along the north edge should be widened and the number of traffic lanes reduced. Perhaps a clearer system of pedestrian crossings with traffic lights should be introduced at the corners of the central space. Perhaps

The elevations of Wilkins' National Gallery show his alternative studies for the end pavilions and his concern to pull the plan forward at the ends. The elevation is very attenuated. It seems beyond question that any addition should avoid further elongating this composition.

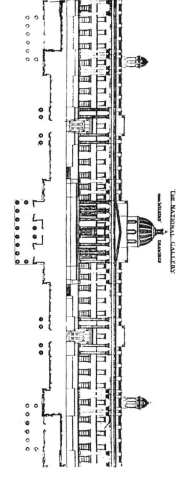

THE NATIONAL GALLERY —WILKINS' DRAWING

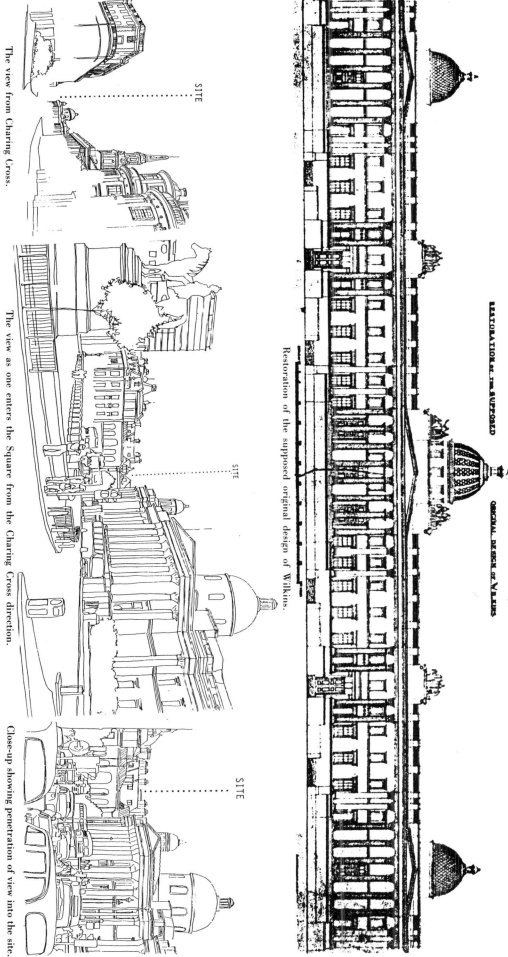

RESTORATION of the SUPPOSED ORIGINAL DESIGN of WILKINS

Wilkins' National Gallery elevation.

Restoration of the supposed original design of Wilkins.

SITE

**Sequence from Charing Cross**
From the forecourt at Charing Cross Station, there is a long view towards the site

The view from Charing Cross.

with a particularly interesting roofscape. In the foreground are Nash's 'pepperpots' with the tower of St Martin's behind, followed by the domes of the National Gallery. This view looks deep into the Hampton site. The composition of the

The view as one enters the Square from the Charing Cross direction.

Wilkins facade works well when foreshortened in perspective.

Close-up showing penetration of view into the site.

**JEREMY DIXON AND BDP**

## Sequence from Pall Mall

Looking down Pall Mall, the Wilkins elevation is tilted in plan to place its main dome on the axis of Pall Mall. As one gets closer to Trafalgar Square, it is possible to see the edge of the site (at present a hoarding). It is at this point that an assessment has to be made as to the bulk of the building that can be appropriately placed in front of the Wilkins elevation.

From the other side of Pall Mall East, as one nears the site, there is what we have identified as a 'favourite view'. The three porticos, Smirke's Royal College of Physicians on the right, the Wilkins Gallery building will become a fourth element in this sequence and should play a similar to St-Martin-in-the-Fields in the distance all come into a charming casual relationship. Each appears to ignore the others like strangers in a crowd. At this point, a row rectangular space, not much wider building on the Hampton site would be on the left but out of sight. However, the new entrance on the left and Gibb's entrance role to the other elements in this informal composition. From this view point, one could imagine Trafalgar Square as a narrow rectangular space, not much wider than the extent of the view shown.

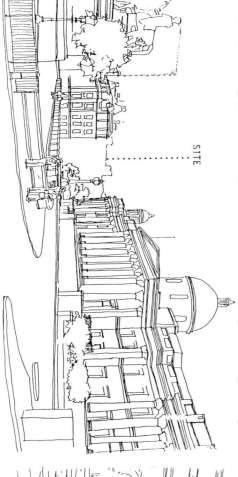

Long view up Pall Mall with the Gallery dome on axis.

SITE

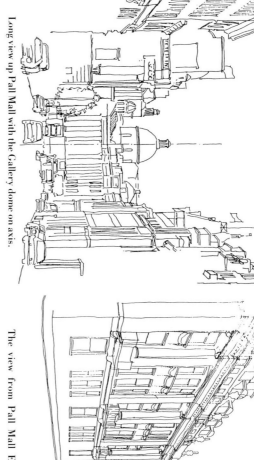

The view from Pall Mall East towards the hoarding.

SITE

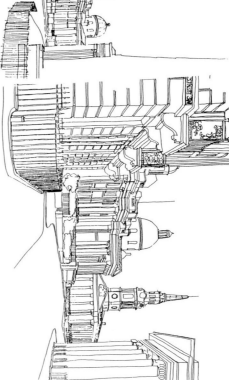

'Favourite view' of the three porticos.

## Sequence from Whitehall

From this direction the ground rises gradually towards the north side of the Square. This tips the foreground up towards the viewer, exaggerating the amount of the ground plane that is visible, particularly the existing Gallery, appear small compared with the monuments within the Square that are in the foreground. Moving northwards across the Square, there is a constantly varying visibility which is a characteristic of the site which presents a different aspect to virtually every angle of view. It means that the consequences of any particular building form have to be checked from all directions and probably need several different ideas for the different situations.

The equestrian statue in front of the Hampton site is missing. It would be very nice to find a suitable piece, maybe a copy of an early Renaissance statue, to occupy the available pedestal.

The site is very visible towards the southeast but drops out of sight altogether on the west side of the Square.

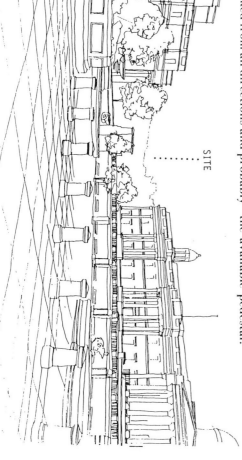

View approaching the National Gallery entrance from the east.

SITE

View from halfway across the Square with missing statue.

## Steps

There is a happy coincidence between the location of various flights of steps along the north edge of the Square and the south-facing orientation that leads to these stepped areas being used as meeting places and as convenient situations to sit

and look at the view across the Square. The point is well illustrated by the stepped base to St-Martin-in-the-Fields, as well as by the flight of steps to the main entrance to the National Gallery. There are also the various shorter flights of steps within the Square itself.

Continuing the sequence from Whitehall northwards, seen as a gently rising progression towards the portico that forms the entrance to the National Gallery, there is a quite different view of the Square looking southwards from the elevation provided by the entrance portico. The

ground is now falling away, bringing the various elements of the view together into a more interesting and coherent picture. From within the portico, there are the views to the left towards St Martin's and to the right towards the visible section of the Hampton site.

View of steps at the base of St Martin's.

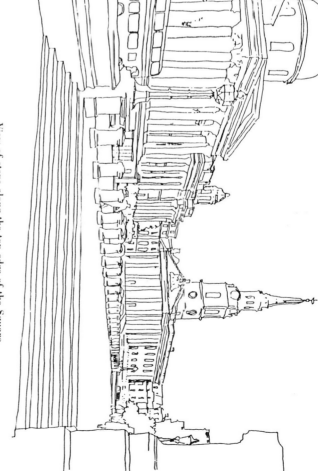

View of steps along the top edge of the Square.

## Trafalgar Square and Leicester Square

The route northwards can be continued along the path between the Hampton site and the existing Gallery that connects Trafalgar Square via St Martin's Street to Leicester Square. This is a moderately important pedestrian link, but significant

in any case as the connection between two principal London public spaces. The ground continues to rise along this route.

The section drawn from Leicester Square to Trafalgar Square suggests the first point of departure towards Trafalgar Square at about the same level as

that a datum is established somewhere around the flank wall to the last extension to the Gallery. A podium is established at this level that takes the pedestrian route between the two squares horizontally, to arrive at an elevated viewpoint overlooking

the present Gallery's main entrance. From here, there would be a dramatic opening up of the view diagonally across the Square with Smirke's fine Greek Revival portico in the foreground.

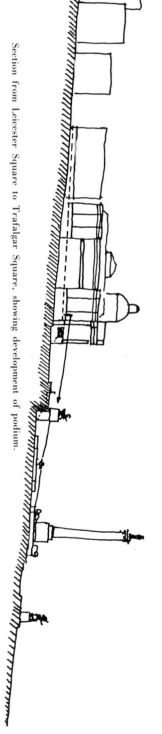

Section from Leicester Square to Trafalgar Square, showing development of podium.

## JEREMY DIXON AND BDP

## The podium and the status of the extension

The podium thus formed would be connected to pavement level along the north side of Trafalgar Square by a broad flight of steps generating a widened pavement zone in front of the Gallery. The present Gallery itself is designed as a building on a podium. The road in front of the Gallery is constantly filled with traffic and is likely to remain so. It is interesting to notice the way the podium to the existing Gallery lifts the main composition of the building above the general level of cars and taxis. The fence in front of the podium to the present Gallery has, except in winter, a characteristic fig hedge that modifies the perception of the podium, leaving the main entrance and side entrances to thrust through and express the full height of the elevation. The project would retain the fig hedge, and the new flight of steps would be a further element projecting through this green line.

The status of an extension on the Hampton site in relation to the existing building is a crucial aspect of the project. The extension can be seen literally as an extension of the existing building, physically continuing the fabric, organisationally continuing the pattern of the existing galleries, and formally emphasising continuity. The alternative is to emphasise the separateness and independent coherence of the

extension as a new and self-contained building with its own front entrance, present National Gallery ideas and formal image.

One of the main arguments for separateness is the tendency for national institutions, such as the National Gallery, simply to grow bigger. There comes a point where the size of a museum building interferes with the enjoyment of visiting it. This happens in two ways. There is the obvious problem of cultural indigestion and not knowing how to control the extent of one's visit. There is also the problem of circulation within a very large building. It becomes necessary to

identify linear routes; in the case of the present National Gallery there appear to be a number of interlinking circular routes that channel the visitor to prescribed destinations. The alternative is well illustrated by a gallery of the size of the Dulwich Picture Gallery. Here the building is comprehensible as a totality. It is not necessary to set out prescribed routes because you can see where you are and you can choose which way to go or what order in which to see the pictures without feeling that an interpretation has been imposed on you. This is obviously a separate identity of the new building.

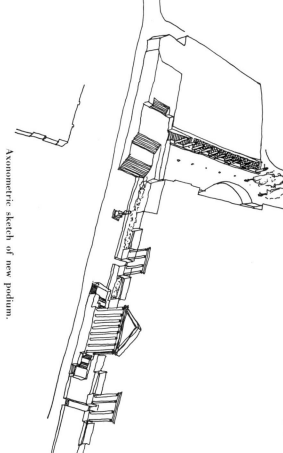

Axonometric sketch of new podium.

## JEREMY DIXON AND BDP

judgement to make in relation to the Early Renaissance Collection and the size of the building on the Hampton site as to whether it is sufficiently limited in size to be able to take advantage of this characteristic of simple directness of plan organisation.

It is our conclusion that the Hampton site building would gain from being seen in as many ways as possible as an independent building standing alongside the present National Gallery but linked to it as a matter of convenience. The two buildings are strongly related whatever one does and it is more a question of how much one 'pulls them apart' and makes the point of separation.

The podium is, therefore, seen as a device on which to place a clearly separate and identifiable object, that is, the new Gallery. It incidentally provides an underlying relationship between the existing Gallery and the new Gallery by way of a base that is common to both. The accommodation required by the gallery, with the actual gallery space filling up the whole site at the top level, makes for a building that is difficult to express in the round as a separate identity, and it was, therefore, an early decision to take part of the new building and pull it out to the front on the podium as a symbol of the new building.

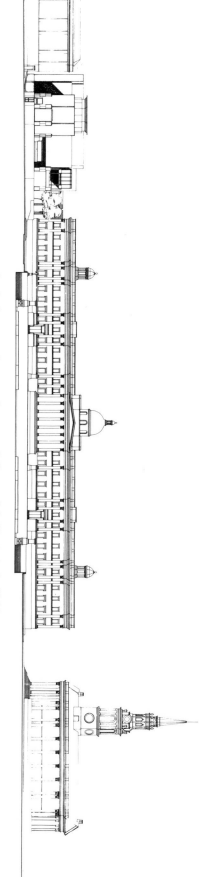

South elevation of new and existing Gallery and St Martin-in-the-Fields.

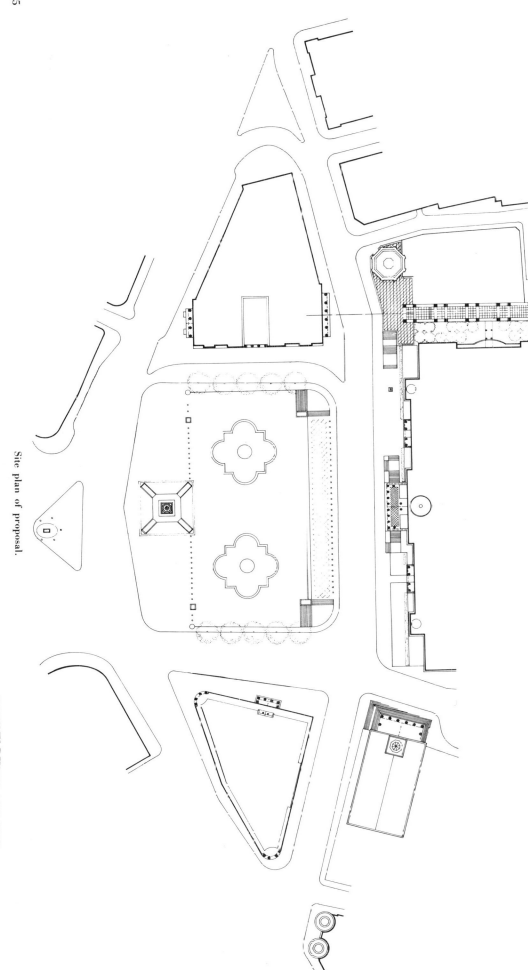

Site plan of proposal.

**JEREMY DIXON AND BDP**

**Organisation of the new gallery building**
The introduction of the podium and main entrance to the new building off the podium generates a section different from that described in the information supplied to competitors. The podium provides a 'piano nobile' at first floor that is detached from the street and its noise and tourist pressure, and can be seen as a focus for accommodation other than the actual galleries. In other words, it provides an entrance level for all the social and less formal functions such as res-taurant, postcards and posters, informa-tion, cloaks, etc, with the more formally organised spaces of the galleries above and the specific functions such as lecture hall and temporary exhibition space be-low. The bookshop proper takes street frontage along Trafalgar Square.

The entrance and a principal gallery above take the form of a separately ex-pressed octagon standing on the podium with the bulk of the building lying behind. A viewing place at gallery level, a baldac-chino, forms the other element on the podium and marks the entrance to the arcade. It is from this corner that there is the best view across Trafalgar Square from the site. The present garden strip is raised to podium level and substantially planted to provide a strong separation between the two buildings as well as an opportunity for views into dappled green light from windows in the new galleries. This strategy reduced the available gal-lery space by not filling the gap between the two buildings with additional gallery space around the bridge, and not building out to the very front line of the site towards Trafalgar Square. However, the galleries developed in the project have the 500m run of wall space required by the brief without using these areas. The pub-lic gestures made by the scheme as a whole, that is, the podium and its view, the steps as a new meeting place, the arcaded route looking into the garden and the garden itself, these gestures are well worth achieving and are the kind of con-tribution that a public building should make to its urban surroundings.

## Circulation

The proposal to build a gallery building with its own entrance alongside the present Gallery necessarily introduces a number of ambiguities into the circulation pattern of each building. We would like the existing main entrance to the Wilkins building to remain the main entrance to the National Gallery. It is placed in such a formally unambiguous position in relation to Trafalgar Square that any suggestion that the main entrance might move seems quite out of place. However, the logical problem remains that the earliest paintings are in the new building. How do people visit the National Gallery? How many set out to see everything? According to the Gallery's own information, only a very small minority visit the whole building. Perhaps the separation of the two entrances will help people to choose to visit the part of the collection they are most interested in. Again, it seems worth emphasising the importance of the relationship between each building and its individual entrance rather than making too much of the ambiguities generated by the connecting link.

The brief for the new building contains a mixture of functions that could be said to be separate and particularly related to the new building, and functions that are clearly part of the Gallery seen as a whole. In the former category we would see shops in this country suggests a high priority in the minds of visitors on browsing, handling books, checking what is in the gallery by looking at postcards, buying Christmas presents etc, that distorts a simple interpretation of the circulation within a gallery as being the

galleries in this country is that the shop can become important in a way that may not seem understandable if the Gallery is seen as primarily a place for contemplation of works of art. The huge commercial success of American gallery shops and the intense interest and activity in gallery way to pulling the main entrance to the whole Gallery into the extension. This does not seem to be a good thing. We would suggest a careful assessment as to whether the shop, or at least part of the entrance sequence to the main Gallery.

In the former category is the restaurant: shops in this country suggests a high priority in the minds of visitors on browsing, handling books, checking what is in the gallery by looking at postcards, buying Christmas presents etc, that distorts a simple interpretation of the circulation within a gallery as being the

## Entrance sequence

The galleries are some two-and-a-half floors up in the air and the problem of reaching them is well illustrated by the activity of viewing paintings which is well achieved by walking up a series of generous flights of steps. The podium provides a break in the sequence of rising from street to gallery level, at which point

move an important aspect of entering a main entrance.) The entrance route is a deliberately prolonged sequence of experiences with zones for reorientation. The sequence can also be seen as part of a gallery lighting idea with the distance between main entrance and stair to gallery level being used as a period of adaptation to lower lighting levels as one approaches the gallery spaces.

progression from entrance to gallery space. In a number of cases in America, extensions to galleries that contain the main entrances, and there is a possibility that moving the shop to be part of the entrance sequence to the extension will go a long way to pulling the main entrance to the whole Gallery into the extension. This does not seem to be a good thing. We would suggest a careful assessment as to whether the shop, or at least part of the entrance sequence to the main Gallery.

Entrance-level plan showing circulation.

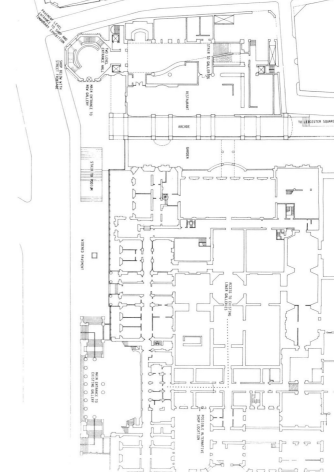

We understand that an entrance at the mezzanine level is being considered to the lower-floor galleries. It might be that part of this entrance sequence could contain an element of the shop directly reached from the first entrance level.

Should the shop remain in the new building, it is part of our proposal that it is accessible directly from street level, as well as podium level.

The temporary exhibition space generates large numbers of visitors at peak periods. Again, there seems to be an argument for allowing direct access from street level to the temporary exhibition space to give the opportunity of avoiding overcrowding the normal entrance sequence to the new Gallery. Diagrammatically the two 'difficult' elements, bookshop and temporary exhibition space, are kept as part of the podium which is symbolically the element that unifies both buildings.

If the shop is kept in the existing building, there may be an argument for keeping the publications department where it is. The present accommodation used by the publications department has very good daylight which will be difficult to match in the new building.

The podium provides an opportunity for a connection between the two buildings for staff circulation at lower level. The circulation pattern between the two sides of the existing lower floors is difficult enough as it is, and there should be convenient connections between the area of the building occupied by the Director, curatorial staff and the library, and the new building. This can take place at lecture hall/temporary exhibition entry level.

at street level is dealt with by a two-level entrance sequence at the base of the octagon. This provides a natural route out past the shop and an identifiable control point if required between octagon and podium-level facilities or perhaps at the base of the stair to the Gallery.

Disabled persons would enter the ground-level entrance, take a lift to

articulation, the present entrance sequence seems a bit abrupt. There is not enough time to understand the next move and orientate yourself. Getting to gallery level in the new building offers a number of possible solutions. One could have an escalator taking the visitor directly to gallery level. However, this seems to re-

there is the main entrance to the building and a view across the Square. Having entered the building, the orientation changes and there is a relaxed progression past the various social activities to a stair up to the galleries towards the back end of the site. (Coming from Leicester Square, the arcade leads naturally to the

The two flights of steps, to the podium and to the existing portico, set up a dialogue between the two entrances and suggest that one route round the whole Gallery involves coming out of one entrance and back in through the other.

The requirement set up in this project for entry at podium level as well as entry

podium level, pass through the control and take a separate lift to gallery level. Wheelchair users who know the Gallery might choose to come along the arcade and through the main entrance, and then by lift to gallery level.

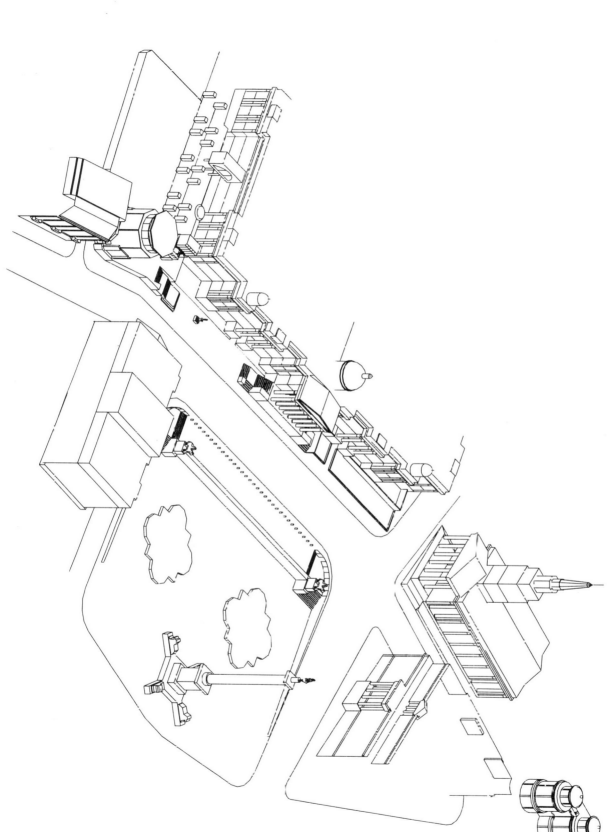

Aerial view showing entrance sequence.

JEREMY DIXON AND BDP

**Design approach: the paintings**

The recent National Gallery Architectural Competition gave rise to much publicity. Most critical discussion was concerned with the external appearance of the proposals and their contribution to Trafalgar Square. However, the project should not be approached simply in terms of the architectural questions surrounding the suitability of buildings for the site: of prime concern must be an appropriate response to the beauty and remarkable quality of the paintings. Here one has an exceptional opportunity to design a new building to house a fixed collection of paintings.

For all practical purposes, the collection is static. A gallery design could be derived entirely from considerations of the arrangement and display of the paintings. This approach, however, will not necessarily take account of the need for the building itself to have strong architectural order and clarity. An approach which relies on the paintings is analogous to the design of a temporary exhibition within an existing space where the enclosures and arrangements need only be influenced by the objects displayed and the circulation requirements. For a permanent gallery building some level of negotiation has to take place between the ordering of the paintings and the coherence of the whole building.

In working on the project, we chose first of all to explore the possibilities of a building directly derived from an interpretation of the 'ideal hang'. To do this, one needs an understanding of the paintings and the reasoning behind the structuring of the ideal hang'. Here we encountered the problem that insight of this kind must necessarily come from the Gallery curators and be part of the development of the project in its next stage. In order to inform ourselves as well as possible and, in a sense, to provide a substitute for the role to be played by the curatorial staff, we talked at length with friends with art historical knowledge of this period, to gain a point of view to work with. It is important that the architect working on the project become deeply involved in the understanding of how the paintings should be displayed. The reasons for hanging paintings in particular arrangements are in part academic and didactic, but also in part a question of visual judgement. The designer should be able to contribute at least to the assessment of visual relationships.

Our first step was to get to know the paintings. We started by mounting colour images, and images to a common scale, of all the 200 or so paintings in the collection, broadly grouping them according to the 'ideal hang'. These were hung round our walls to familiarise ourselves with the whole collection. We then worked on diagrams generated by the 'ideal hang' to see if they suggested building plan arrangements. At the same time studies were done of room sizes in relation to the groups within the 'ideal hang'.

We soon reached the conclusion that the relatively large number of small rooms suggested by the brief would need a larger space to serve as a central ordering device to hold the plan together. Here is an example of a way in which architectural requirements modify a straightforward interpretation of the hang. Likewise, as we have worked on the project, we have increasingly found that aspects of the building suggest changes in the hang arrangements. By definition, without the involvement of the Gallery, this process cannot be drawn to a conclusion. However, we can demonstrate some of the possible lines of development.

**The 'ideal hang'**

The categories within the ideal hang are defined in radically different ways: there are general categories such as centuries, schools, tendencies such as Italian Gothic, and individual artists. The chronology is complicated; Italian Gothicising overlaps well into the periods of time identified in other categories with the Renaissance. Similarly, the developments in different areas of Northern Italy overlap with one another. In other words, it is not a simple matter of comparing the chronology of Northern European Early Renaissance with that of the South. Nonetheless, the special feature of the collection is the unusually good balance of high-quality paintings from Northern Europe and Italy, and the basic ordering of the new galleries should reflect this broad division.

These diagrams illustrate stages in one's understanding of the implications of the ideal hang. They also become the basis for the schemes; the first two generate the the early schemes, the third is the basis of the current proposal.

**Diagram 1**

This is very close to the ideal hang set out in the brief. Broadly it suggests a continuous chronology: Pre-Renaissance is divided from the Renaissance by the vertical dotted line. The diagram is, in fact, inaccurate in that the chronology cannot be simplified to this extent: paintings contemporary with each other occur on either side of this dividing line. Also the simplification into three parallel lines suggests similarity in the lines of development which cannot be substantiated. In other words the diagram is inflexible in certain respects, and over-specific in others.

**Diagram 2**

Here the diagram is divided into four groups. Parallel chronology is replaced by locating these groups around a central area, allowing broad comparisons to be drawn between all of the groups. While it is possible for each group to develop as an intimate set of interrelated gallery spaces, it is difficult to break the system where the broad groupings require modification to accommodate particular paintings or individual painters.

**Diagram 3**

In this case, the various categories overlap one another (in the form of a set diagram). This allows for individual painters and groups to be seen as belonging to more than one category at the same time. For example, Uccello and Fra Angelico are seen as belonging to both the Florentine School and to Italian Gothicising. The remaining paintings in the Italian Gothicising section are identified with the Sienese School, which in turn relates to the Duecento and Trecento through Duccio, Ugolino and Lorenzetti. Pisanello here is an exception; he related well visually to Uccello and to the International Gothic Movement. Lorenzo Monaco, on the other hand, is in both the Sienese and International Gothic category. This suggests a gallery idea in which there is great flexibility during the design process and to some extent after completion of the building to allow for quite subtle adjustments of the hang which would be developed in discussion with the Gallery's curatorial staff. The more sophisticated interconnections between various groups of paintings suggested by this diagram require a gallery layout that is not dependent on simple linear circulation routes. One possible advantage of the size of the new building is that it can cope with a more complex organisation while remaining comprehensible.

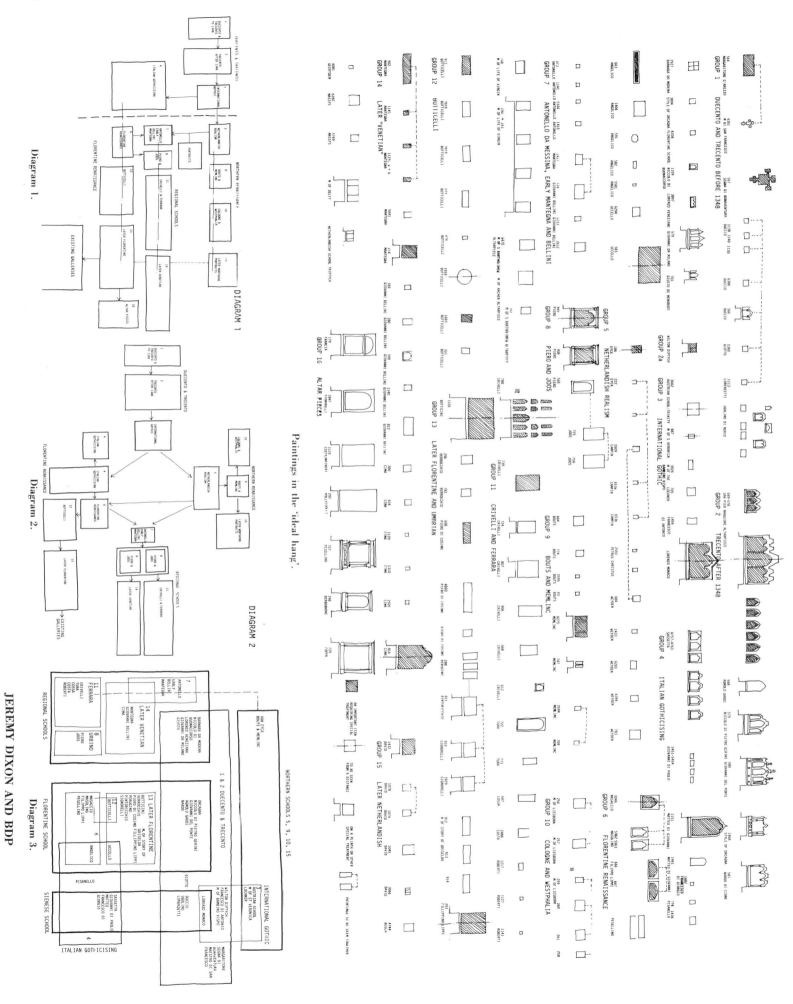

**JEREMY DIXON AND BDP**

Diagram 1.

DIAGRAM 1

Diagram 2.

DIAGRAM 2

Diagram 3.

Paintings in the 'ideal hang'.

# Gallery proposal

The current scheme for the galleries is a development of hang diagram 3. A more disciplined structural idea based on a double grid is used to generate a series of large and small spaces that allow the paintings to be grouped in a more relaxed and 'overlapping' manner. The aim is to fix the main components of the building while leaving the detailed interconnection and grouping of spaces open to discussion and development, as ideas for different painting arrangements arise during the briefing and design discussions. The intention is not to provide any form of tention in use other than in the long term, but rather to allow the building to evolve during the design process.

The basic arrangement of the galleries remains that of a main central 'basilica' space, with Northern paintings on one side and Italian paintings on the other. The stair is now at the end of the long gallery from the octagon. The bridge from the existing building leads into the space allocated to Florentine paintings and the galleries along the garden edge.

The central space acts as a hall between the Italian and Northern Schools and as an introduction to the collection; it contains Duecento and Trecento works. The schools are grouped regionally around these galleries. The smaller rooms between these galleries accommodate paintings which overlap different groups or make connections between groups.

While one cannot reconstruct original locations, one can hint at the implications of precise locations where they are known. For instance, the Pisa altar could hang high on the wall at the correct height for the perspective system within the painting.

In another sense the central gallery could be devoted to altarpieces as a more general category, with the early paintings in the narrow strip to the west, the Italian paintings in the broader strip to the east, and the Northern paintings in the small galleries along the garden edge. The octagon at the end holds the later altarpieces.

The run of galleries along the garden edge provides a second unifying element. The central gallery in this case is seen as accommodating the early paintings, the first two categories in the ideal hang, which consist mostly of gilded altarpieces.

## Accommodating the paintings

Using the basic distribution described above, the drawing looks at a painting arrangement for part of the Gallery. The area chosen is based on the Florentine group, which needs to be adjacent to the bridge to make the necessary connection with paintings in the existing Gallery. The painting.

The grid idea is itself flexible and we have included some of the variants looked at during the development of the present scheme. This gallery layout is flexible in School of paintings.

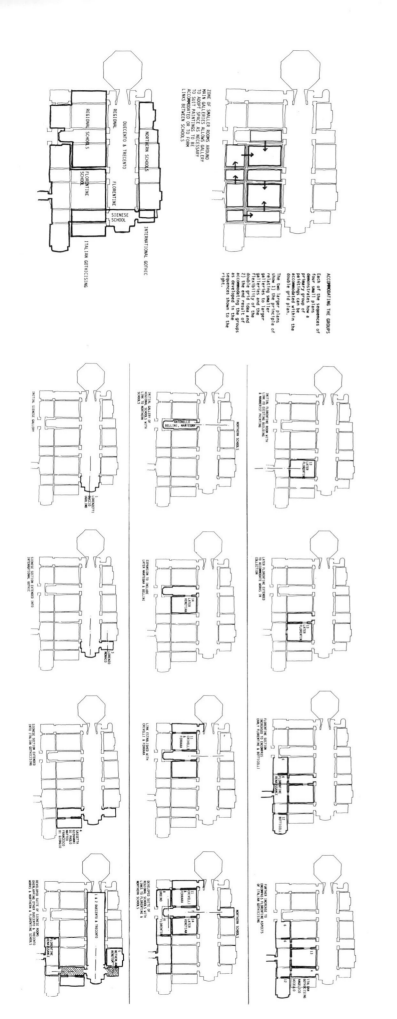

ACCOMMODATING THE GROUPS

Each of the sequences of four small plans demonstrates how a primary group of paintings can be accommodated within the double grid plan.

The two larger plans show: 1) the principle of relating smaller galleries to larger galleries to give flexibility of the double grid idea and 2) the end result of accommodating the groups in sequences shown to the right.

ZONE OF SMALLER ROOMS AROUND MAIN GALLERIES ALLOWING GALLERY TO ADOPT SPACE AS NECESSARY TO SUIT PAINTINGS TO BE ACCOMMODATED OR TO FORM LINKS BETWEEN SCHOOLS

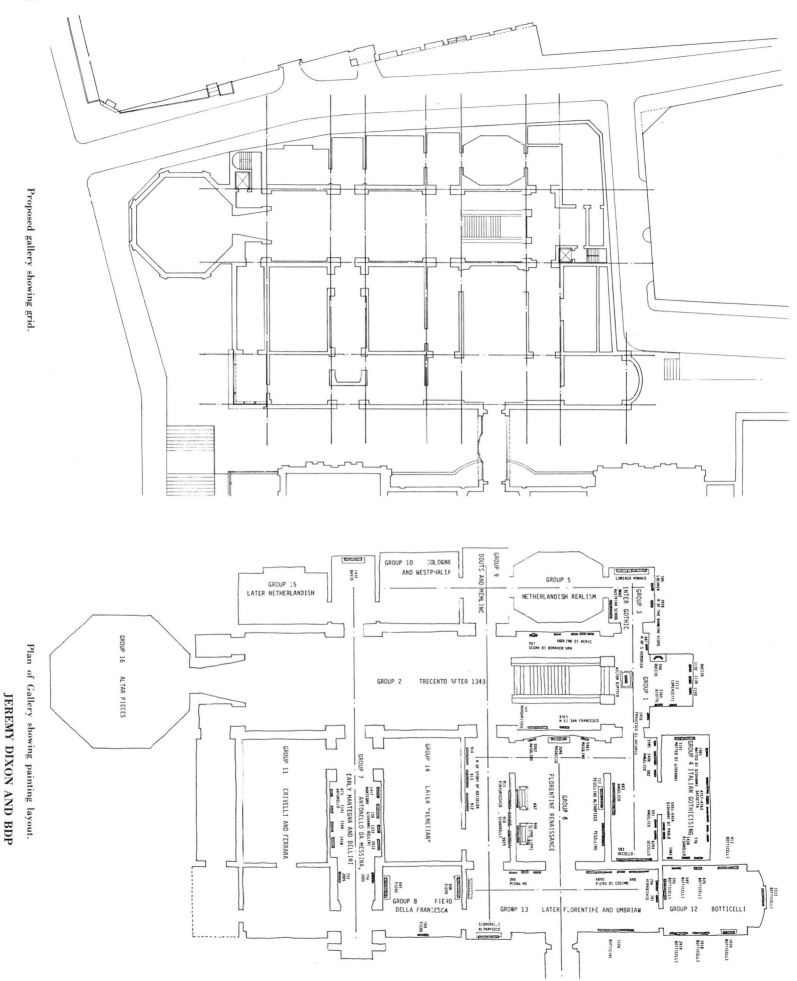

Proposed gallery showing grid.

Plan of Gallery showing painting layout.

**JEREMY DIXON AND BDP**

# Lighting and the gallery sections

he drawing illustrates the galleries within the cross-section of the building. The barrel vaulted main central space has smaller galleries for the Northern paintings on one side and medium-sized galleries for the major Italian groups on the other, with a connected series of smaller galleries adjacent to the garden.

The galleries are formed as enclosures that are separate from the weathertight skin of the building, allowing a first level of control of daylight as part of the glazed roof system, and a second level of control as part of the gallery enclosure. The quality of the interior spaces of the gallery is a matter of proportion and materials but above all else of light.

The lighting in the present galleries is a problem. Daylight is controlled and reduced to the point where the laylights might as well be illuminated artificially for the extent to which daylight can be perceived as coming from them. This leads to an even, dull light that is unflattering to the paintings and generally dulling to the senses. The difficulty is to maintain lighting levels on paintings that are consistent with conservation, ie, around 200 lux, while at the same time enlivening the interior of the gallery with the varying qualities of daylight. The two criteria are in direct opposition to each other. One resolution of the problem is to use daylight to illuminate the fabric of the building where variation in intensity does not matter, and to use artificial light to keep the paintings at a constant level of brightness. This is what Kahn did at the Kimbell Art Gallery at Fort Worth and is broadly what Scarpa did at the Castelvecchio Museum at Verona. Both of these galleries, and in particular the Kimbell Gallery, seem to be almost universally liked and to provide a good gallery experience.

Our approach has been to accept that the galleries are lit by a combination of artificial light on the paintings and carefully directed daylight on the building. The overall lighting ideas for the new gallery are related to the circulation sequence from the main entrance onwards. From full daylight outside on the podium the visitor enters a daylit entrance hall and then moves to a predominantly artificially lit approach to the stair up to the gallery. At this stage daylight would be perceivable in the distance where the restaurant looks onto the garden. The level of lighting drops towards the

the stair so that the eye is accustomed to a low level of illumination well before arriving at the main gallery. This gallery is seen as a space from which most daylight has been excluded, save for the odd shaft of direct sun on the floor at particular times of day, and a small amount of diffused daylight. The early altarpieces are, therefore, in a lofty basilica space lit by artificial light. This will particularly suit the gilding. To each side of this long gallery, the other galleries have a combination of directed daylight and artificial light, with the edge against the garden making use of views into trees that excludes the sky, as an additional component of the experiences of daylight. In other words the experiences of daylight, ie, building is darker in the middle and tends towards light nearer the edge.

The daylighting of the galleries other than the central gallery can be seen in the following manner. Dulwich Picture Gallery has daylight modelling the top half of the gallery space but is marred by the brightness of the actual source, the lanterns. Our lighting consultant, who was the consultant to SOM in the earlier competition, used at the time a specialised ceiling grid with the capacity to direct light very precisely on walls as required. At the time this device was to be used to illuminate the paintings at 150 lux. However, the same device could be used to direct a delicate daylight quality on to the top half of the gallery space. This light source could be allowed to vary in intensity from, say 0-400 lux, depending on outside conditions and direction of sunlight. This device could, therefore, replace the lantern source at Dulwich with what would be a low-brightness ceiling while retaining the daylight effect on the walls. The level light on the paintings would be maintained at 200 lux by artificial light sources. This technique has the advantage of being able to accommodate the wide variety of gallery size that we have in the project, together with subtle gradations of the relative intensity of daylight to artificial light.

**Section B-B.**

GROUP 11 CRIVELLI AND FERRARA — GROUP 7 ANTONELLO DA MESSINA, — GROUP 14 LATER "VENETIAN" — GROUP 13 LATER FLORENTINE — GROUP 6 FLORENTINE RENAISSANCE — GROUP 4 ITALIAN GOTHICISING

**Section C-C.**

VIEWING PLATFORM — GROUP 11 CRIVELLI AND FERRARA — GROUP 8 PIERO DELLA FRANCESCA AND JOOS — GROUP 13 LATER FLORENTINE — GROUP 12 BOTTICELLI

**Section D-D.**

GROUP 5 NETHERLANDISH REALISM — GROUP 1 DUECENTO AND TRECENTO BEFORE 1348 — GROUP 6 FLORENTINE RENAISSANCE — GROUP 13 LATER FLORENTINE — GALLERY 9

**Section E-E.**

GROUP 10 COLOGNE AND WESTPHALIA — GROUP 2 TRECENTO AFTER 1348 — GROUP 14 LATER "VENETIAN" — GROUP 8 PIERO

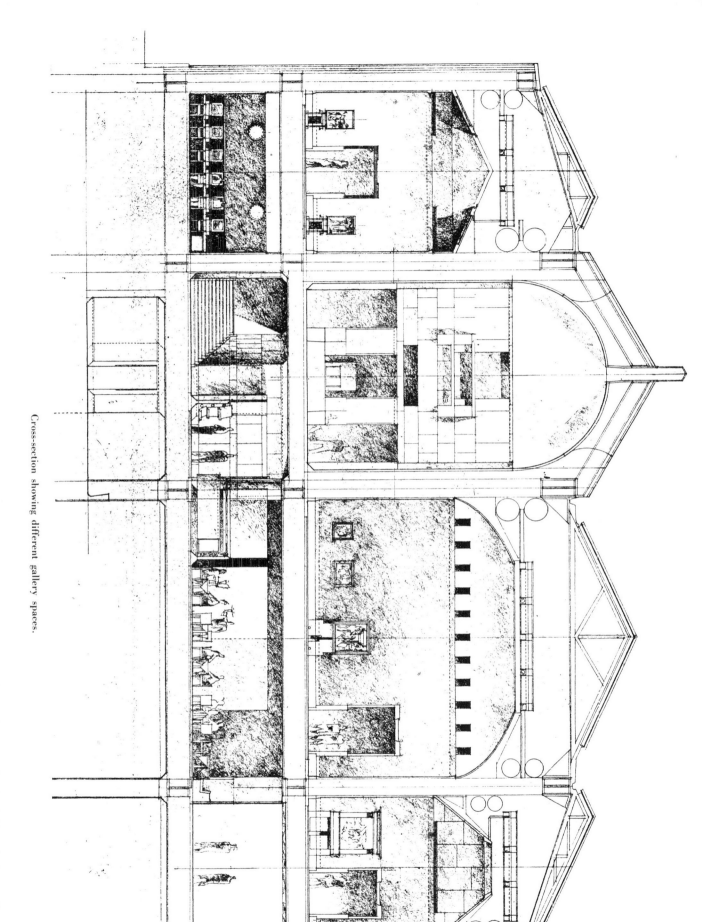

Cross-section showing different gallery spaces.

Galleries for Northern School — small-scale, more domestic, wooden floors, lower door openings, some wooden ceilings, cooler light.

Central space — large-scale, formal, stone floor and wall, paintings in niches and on plinths held away from the walls, acoustic plaster barrel ceiling, balcony on end wall is lobby to boardroom suite.

Principal Italian galleries — formal, more daylight, carpet floor with stone border, toned plaster walls for hanging zone, white acoustic plaster modelled ceiling to emphasise daylight.

Smaller Italian galleries—small-scale, formal, individual — special stone ceiling in example shown horizontal views into trees, toned hanging zone, stone/marble door surrounds, carpet floor with stone border.

**JEREMY DIXON AND BDP**

## Plan at podium level

The main entrance leads to a circular hall within the octagon, linked to the lower the site. The garden is planted with trees over the lower entrance looks in the direction of Pall Mall. This entrance hall is treated as a large-scale draught lobby and reorientation space. Coming through the hall into the main interior space, ahead to the left is the cloakroom and further on to the right the information desk and sales point for cards and posters. Opposite this is the information room seen as a space continuous with the main space, partially screened with glass. Ahead is a broad flight of steps that rises compressing the spatial sense against the ceiling at the half landing where the direction of the stair returns and the upper flight of the staircase to the the gallery above. Along the arcade and taking advantage of the corner towards

the terrace is the restaurant. The kitchen and loading bay are at the north end of towards Pall Mall leads to a two-storey entrance by two flights of steps. A window to give a canopy at gallery level. The quality of light at arcade level will be that of dappled sunlight.

The loading bay is based on a medium-sized delivery lorry. It would be a matter for discussion with the Gallery exactly what size of lorry should be accommodated. The loading bay gives access to the kitchen and to the picture room. Along one side is the car lift to the basement parking area.

The two lifts either side of the entrance connect to the levels below and a separate lift goes up to the gallery allowing the possibility of a control point between the two. The lift beyond the staircase to the suite at roof level.

## Plan at pavement level

The pavement-level entrance facing back either side of the entrance and a series of windows linking with the main podium entrance. In one direction is the bookshop and in the other the approach to the temporary exhibition hall and the sub-divisible lecture room. On the left are toilets, cloaks and accommodation for warders. At the end is a room for the Friends with the potential for overlooking the two-storey exhibition space. There is lift access from the entrance at this level both to the podium level and the temporary exhibition room level for the disabled. At the north end of the building and under the garden is a perimeter service zone allowing air to be taken in around the area that gives light to the restoration level.

workshops.

The bookshop has display windows windows locking directly into the selling space.

The direct entrance from the street to the temporary exhibition space may well be of some advantage particularly when popular exhibition is on. The hall provides plenty of queuing space and the extra traffic in the building will not be imposed on what should be a calm atmosphere in the accommodation on the podium above.

Staff circulation between the new building and the existing building takes place at pavement level via the bookshop, with an additional route at basement level.

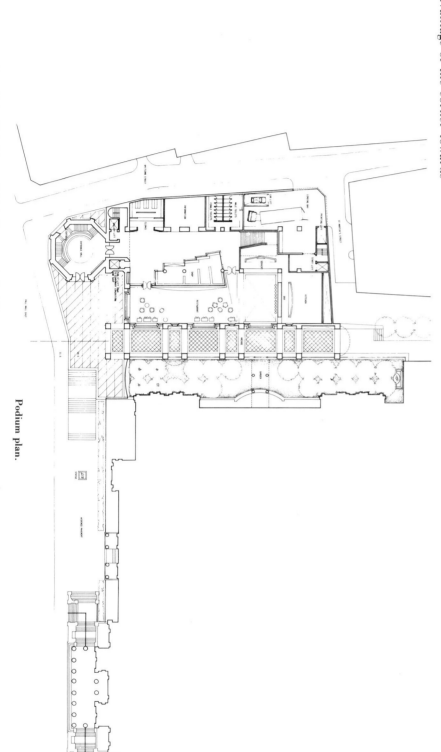

Podium plan.

**Plan at gallery level**

The plan allows for various categories of gallery space. The largest space is the central gallery into which the stair from the entrance sequence rises. The medium-sized galleries to the east of the central gallery and their related smaller spaces are seen as one group, the Italian paint-ings. The smaller spaces to the west of the central gallery are a separate group de-voted to the Northern paintings.

There is an opportunity to vary the atmosphere and general 'feel' of the gal-lery spaces from one category to another. This is achieved by a combination of lighting, materials and acoustics. The ex-tent of the variation has to be carefully controlled so that the new building as a whole retains a unity while there is an interesting and appropriate range of ex-periences and appropriate locations for the paintings. The plan shows a variety of floor finishes. The zone around the edge of galleries to discourage visitors from approaching the paintings is defined by a horizontal stone or marble skirting that forms a border to each room and a threshold zone between rooms. At the edge of this zone would be recessed sock-ets for rope supports, should they be necessary. 'The actual floor finishes with-in the gallery spaces follow the categories above with the Northern gallery having woodblock floor in appropriate patterns, the central gallery having a stone floor, and the Italian galleries having carpeted floors. This leads to an interesting change of resilience as one walks across the width of the building from carpet to stone to wood. At the same time, the acoustic quality of the rooms will vary with the floor finishes. (The acoustic report sug-gests that the aspect of the rooms that will give the greatest variety to acoustic quali-ty is the floor finish.)

'The walls of the gallery spaces will generally be a painted plaster or acoustic finish, to allow for simple repair and redecoration when paintings are moved or lent. The exception is the long central gallery which will have stone walls. Most of the paintings in this area will be on plinths and the problems asso-ciated with hanging paintings on stonework will not arise. The hang zone in galleries generally will have a darkish tone, either neutral or coloured, to contrast with the ceiling zone which will be white to pick up the varying daylight falling across the top portion of the gallery space.

The lighting varies with the cross-section, with the central gallery having a lower level of illumination and less day-light, with a sense of increasing daylight as one moves towards the edge of the building. Along the site adjacent to the garden, a series of small galleries presents the opportunity for limited areas of win-dow looking into the trees. The level of light from this kind of source would be compatible with looking at the paintings. At the Trafalgar Square end of this range of galleries is a room outside the gallery spaces that takes advantage of the view across the Square. This would have to have a careful adjustment of the screen-ing of daylight to allow the eye to adjust back to gallery level reasonably quickly. Similarly, the bridge between the build-ings provides an opportunity to look into the garden space and at the same time to give a clear sense of separation between the two buildings. The range of galleries along the garden edge provides a second 'ordering device' similar to the central gallery but of a lesser order, for the bridge connection to the new building to arrive at.

The door surrounds and skirtings are of stone or marble and are a unifying element across the gallery.

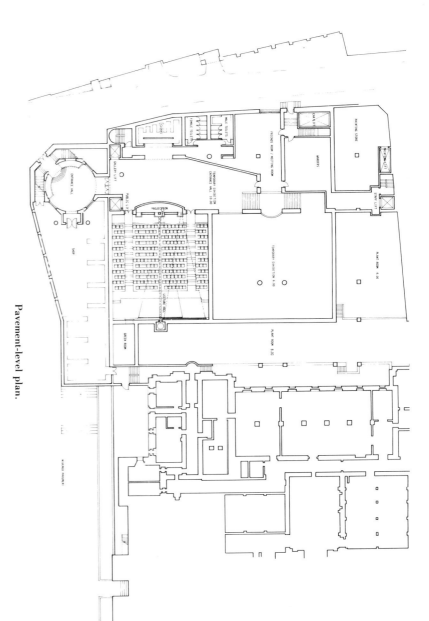

Pavement-level plan.

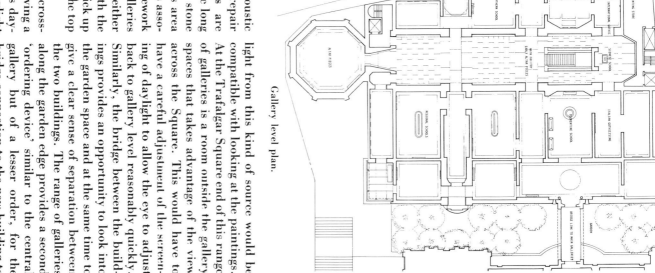

Gallery level plan.

**JEREMY DIXON AND BDP**

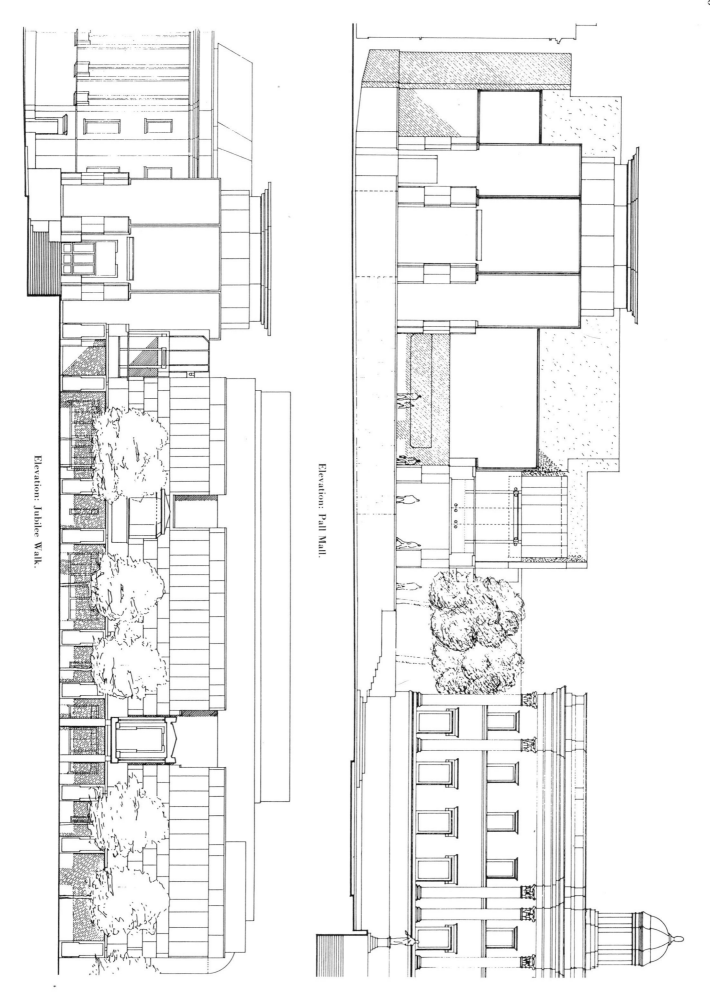

Elevation: Jubilee Walk.

Elevation: Pall Mall.

JEREMY DIXON AND BDP

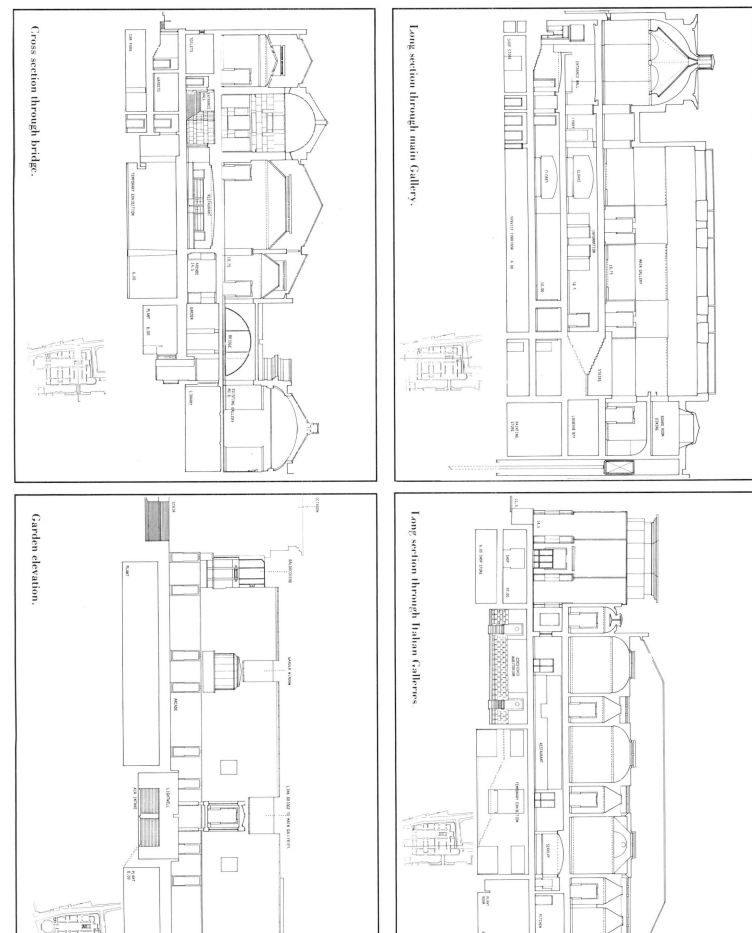

27

Cross section through bridge.

Long section through main Gallery.

Garden elevation.

Long section through Italian Galleries.

JEREMY DIXON AND BDP

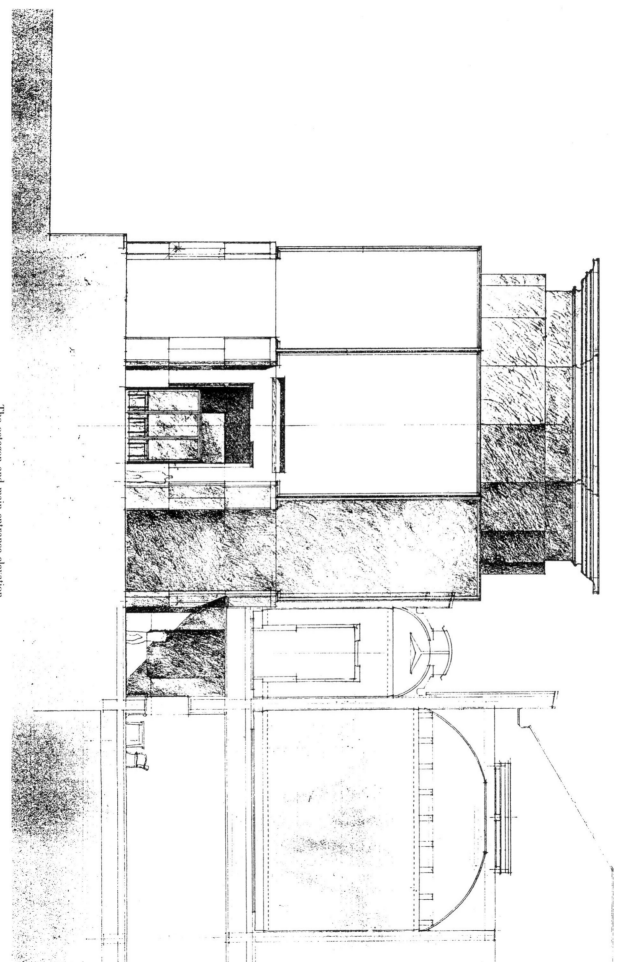

The octagon and main entrance elevation.

JEREMY DIXON AND BDP

**Studies of the external elevation — the octagon and main entrance**
The external walls of the building generally are of stone. The octagon and the various features visible on the podium from Trafalgar Square require the most careful treatment. The proposal is to use two colours of stone, whitish Portland stone and the creamy yellow Bath stone, rather in the manner of the recently

cleaned Smirke portico opposite. The detailing of the stonework should not overemphasise the thickness and articulation of the surface. There is a quality difficult to describe in both the Greek Revival buildings and the rendering of buildings in the 'ideal perspectives' of the Renaissance period that gives to the faces of three-dimensional forms a thinness and restraint of modelling that we would like

to imitate.
The materials of the podium and floor are important. There is an opportunity for geometric patterning of the floor surface that becomes visible from the viewing gallery above.

**Studies of the external elevation — the viewing gallery**
The viewing gallery at the southeast cor-

ner of the new building takes advantage of the best view across the Square. It takes the form of a metal, glass and alabaster baldacchino. This and the octagon are the main expressive elements on the podium. The octagon marks the main entrance to the new building and the baldacchino sits over the entrance to the arcade.

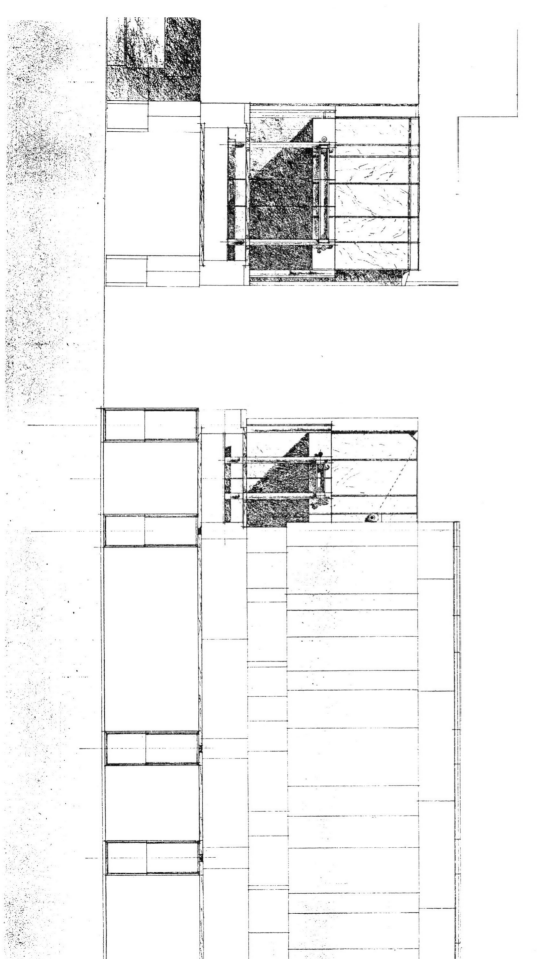

The viewing gallery elevation.

**JEREMY DIXON AND BDP**

**Imagery of the octagon**

The octagon was chosen in the early studies for the project as an appropriate form to relate to the style of the Wilkins elevation and the Smirke elevation, both being Greek Revival buildings, and the octagon being a 'Temple of the Winds'. As we have worked on the project, the octa-

gon has been seen in other ways as a suitable symbol for the new building.

The Gibbs Mausoleum suggests the use of the form for mausoleums: the mausoleum has an appropriateness as a building reminding one of the importance of the past.

The Brunelleschi perspective of the

Florence Baptistry suggests the use of the form for baptistries: the reference to the kind of drawing in that it consists of a baptistry is appropriate in relation to the variety of 'palazzo' type buildings unusual in London.

The sketches of various British Temple of the Winds examples were our studies for the first versions of the octagon on the

street that can be associated with this paintings housed and particularly the large altarpieces in the octagonal room.

The partial view of Piero's ideal perspective suggests the use of polygonal buildings in the street scene. Pall Mall is a podium.

Gibbs: Mausoleum.

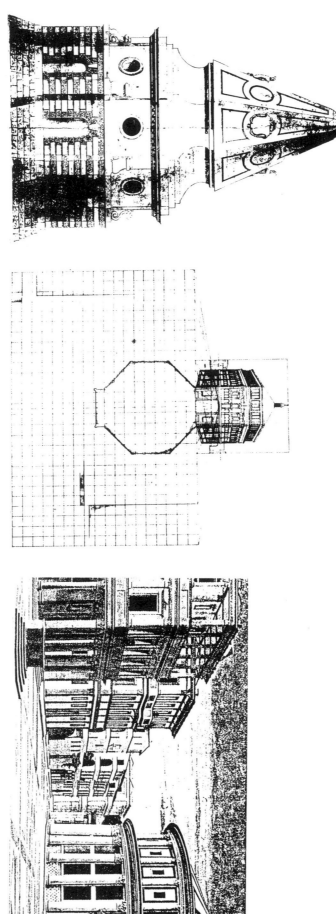

Brunelleschi: Florence Baptistry.

Temple of the Winds sketches.

Piero: street scene.

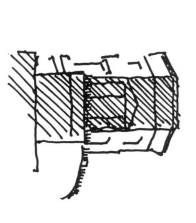

Jeremy Dixon
William Jack of BDP
Alan Baxter Associates
BDP
Gardiner & Theobald
George Sexton Associates
BDP Acoustics
BDP Landscape

— Architects
— Structure
— M&E Services
— QS Services
— Lighting
— Acoustics
— Landscape

All the above consultancy firms have made a contribution to this submission.

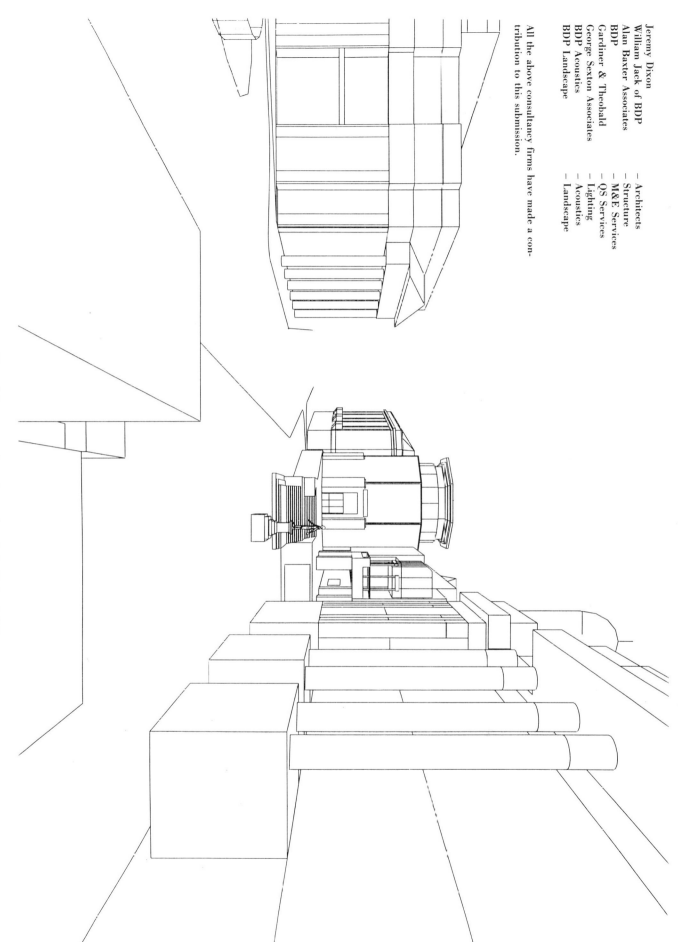

View of the octagon from the portico of the National Gallery.

JEREMY DIXON AND BDP

# Campbell Zogolovitch Wilkinson & Gough

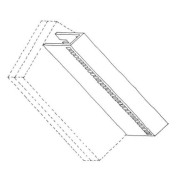

## Derivation of form

The overall arrangement of the extension has been determined by the design of the gallery rooms, all other spaces being subservient to their structural and other requirements. Thus the building is designed from the top downwards.

The grand Victorian rooms of the existing gallery or their modern equivalents (eg, the Neue Pinakothek in Munich) do not make good models for hanging early pictures. The atmosphere of great palaces and boudoirs is too lush for the purity of these paintings. Other types of more modern space with laylights and newer more contrived versions of the same tend to be oppressive and heavy, particularly where the natural light source is made to seem artificial by processing and sieving it of life. Side lighting makes spaces more pleasant and natural, but has the problem of reflections.

The idea of a basilica brought up in the previous competition therefore seems to be a most apt exemplar for galleries to house Early Renaissance paintings. One envisages a long high space of simple form that our design is developed from. A 63m (207ft) long central axis gallery is proposed running the full length of the site. To this are added at right angles slightly lower and narrower side galleries, being the ideal hanging for pictures, although some later Dutch paintings of

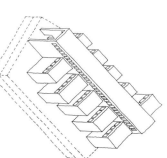

church interiors might persuade one otherwise.

The requirement for hanging pictures without reflections demands a daylight source from above an angle of about 45°. Many recent articles and books explain ways in which this may be achieved by the use of lanterns, laylights and internal and external reflection baffles.

Usually the object of the exercise is to reduce the overall height of the construction and make the light as even as possible. In fact, buildings remain high with volumes of concealed space for control systems which are not perceptible to the viewer except when, worst of all, the whole ghastly affair is on view.

These solutions are often diagramatically compared with the greater height required for simple clerestory daylighting from the top of the opposite wall of a room.

This requires a space roughly twice as high as it is wide. Spiritually, this form is an ideal one in which to hang Early Renaissance pictures. It is therefore this form that our design is developed from.

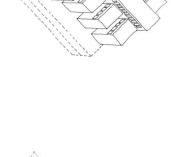

directly by doorways from the main space and linked to each other as well.

The groups of Northern paintings are ranged down the west side and Italian down the east. The rooms vary in size to accommodate the different collections. The central space houses a number of groups, particularly those central to the development of Renaissance painting and those relating to both North and South.

The intrinsic configuration of this arrangement is such that a visitor may quickly grasp the simplicity of organisation of the arrangement. He should be able to perceive the scale of the whole extension and pace his progress accordingly. The point of arrival on the gallery floor should coincide for visitors from the existing Gallery and the new extension at the entry to Gallery 1. This is placed as a prelude to the main axis galleries, as its contents are separated historically by the Black Death.

A bridge link to the existing Gallery 9 on its central axis is the most logical. Thus the visitors arriving at the extension can make their way to the rest of the gallery should they wish.

At the end of the sequence of galleries, the visitor is at the south end of the building. An enclosed glazed loggia giving marvellous views over Trafalgar Square

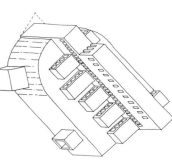

makes a delightful way to perambulate back to the staircase, lifts and bridge.

A semicircular form had already been perceived as a good way of solving the forward projection of a building on the site. It makes an excellent termination of the corner of the Square. It also disguises the awkwardness of the shape of the site.

Finally, the side lighting of the galleries makes it possible to stand an additional attic storey on the top of the central space. This is a good place for the boardroom, dining and committee rooms where they can be top lit without taking gallery-level space or competing with public use and enjoyment of views over Trafalgar Square on the floors which are accessible to the public.

Thus the major block forms of the building are defined. A drum-shaped form is intersected by a long high rectangular block. The new extension is separated from the old to allow windows in both and the Jubilee Walk to pass through without dividing the ground floor. The best place for the new entrance is at the junction of this realigned Jubilee Walk and the Pall Mall East pavement, where it can be seen from all directions of approach. Its accessibility for elderly and disabled people makes this visibility more than desirable.

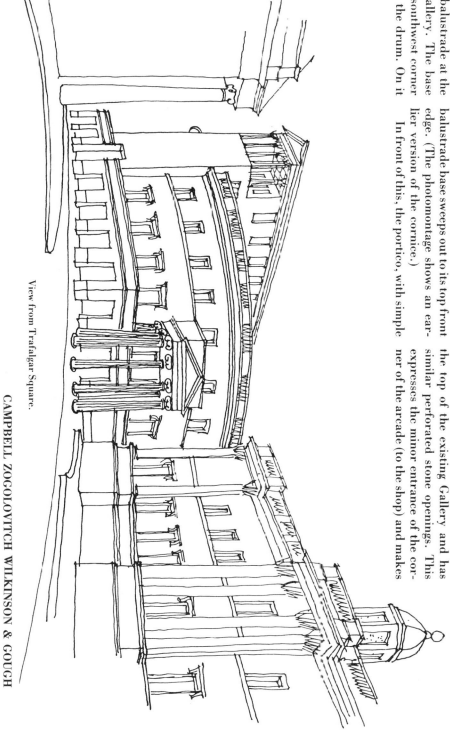

View from Trafalgar Square.

CAMPBELL ZOGOLOVITCH WILKINSON & GOUGH

At this stage of development the appearance of the building could still take many forms. A straightforward continuation of the vocabulary of the existing building, with base, cornice and portico derived directly from the Wilkins facade, would result in an appearance somewhat in the manner of Alexander 'Greek' Thompson.

The portico steps down off the base onto the pavement and is echoed in the attic storey, while the drum is punctuated by windows on the first and second floors. However, the latter were felt not to express adequately the potential for much larger areas of glazing in the drum than would be easily accommodated by another Greek Revival. Also there was a desire to respond architecturally to the nature of the collection to be housed.

Thus in the present design, the grammar of the existing building is followed but the vocabulary is different. There is a base and a cornice and balustrade at the levels of the existing Gallery. The base follows the site into the southwest corner and around the base of the drum. On it stand the tall rectangular block, the drum, and a turret on the corner. The rectangular block has a south face of sheer unbroken stone with one blind opening at the top to represent its nature as a gallery. It is surmounted by the open end of the barrel-shaped roof of the board-room floor forming a vaulted covered portico. The inverted cornice at this level is similar to the base of the dome on the main building. (This part is of similar height and alignment to the Sun Life Building on the south side of Pall Mall East.)

The drum of the building facing the Square is chiefly of glass in shallow flutes divided by stone pilasters. The face of both materials would be flush with each other so that they read as a surface, not as a wall. The projecting cornice itself is supported by large single dentils at the top of the pilasters, while the balustrade base sweeps out to its top front edge. (The photomontage shows an earlier version of the cornice.)

In front of this, the portico, with simple Tuscan columns befitting their lower station, supports an external staircase which leads down from the gallery floor to the restaurant floor below and has its halfway landing on the side overlooking the Square, making another slightly higher viewing position to that of the existing portico. The double-arched pediment repeats the head of the blind opening below the attic balcony. The underside of the lower part of the staircase slopes down from the soffit of the portico to the top of the entrance door in a double bracket supported halfway by the inner columns which are thus lower and in false perspective. These brackets, the soffit and the underside of the coffered attic balcony are painted the blue of the clock of St-Martin-in-the-Fields, which goes so beautifully with Portland stone.

The turret on the southwest corner is a distant relation of the octagonal ones on the top of the existing Gallery and has similar perforated stone openings. This expresses the minor entrance of the corner of the arcade (to the shop) and makes a less heroic aspect of the building to Pall Mall East.

The other most important view of the building is down St Martin's Street from Leicester Square. The northeast corner of the building has a semicircular tower to house an escape stair, a small glazed loggia and, lower down, the car lift, this element being slightly behind the North Wing extension indicating a way past on that side, while the north wall itself is perhaps plainer – suggesting that it is the back of a building.

The Jubilee Walk will now be in the rather dramatic space between the old and new buildings, crossed by a large and a small bridge. The east flank wall of the extension is articulated by a number of the shallow flutes in stone, windows to the offices on the first floor, and the cornice and base which continue around the building.

## Ground-floor plan

The building is entered by the portico in front of the southwest corner of the main Gallery. The entrance doors are central and project forward from the line of the base; the glass sliding doors are protected at night by outward opening steel ones. The exit doors are less prominent to one side and have inward opening outer doors. A weather lobby, with a security room adjacent, leads into a circular entrance hall 17m (56ft) in diameter on plan with a double-height space of 8m (26ft) through a central circular opening to the first floor. Columns rise from the edge of this opening (as the floor is in fact hung from above to reduce columns on the ground floor). From the entrance hall the major public functions of the building can be perceived. A large grand curving staircase projects into the space and leads up to the gallery floor. Straight ahead on entry are the Gallery guides and information, a most important aspect of the visitors' understanding and enjoyment of their visit. Many appear to be discouraged by overcrowding from consulting the present guides and thus embark on an aimless walk around. We propose four guides as well as posters and other information. A small booth has been allowed for a person to answer questions and dispense free literature.

To the left on entering the cloakroom, which to save ground-floor space is equipped with a paternoster retrieval system allowing coats and bags to be left or collected at either this counter or the theatre foyer below. The bookshop has a 9m (30ft) frontage to the hall with fold-away glazing and doors, to be opened or retained depending on the level of security required. The bookshop may also be entered from the street via the arcade on the southwest corner. The arcade makes it possible to have large display windows for merchandise without a commercial appearance directly on the street which would be out of character as there are no other shops on this part of Pall Mall East. The arcade might have to be gated at night.

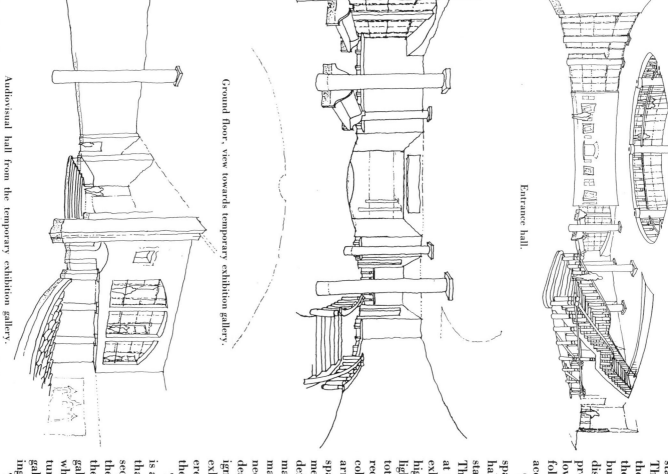

Ground floor, view towards temporary exhibition gallery.

Entrance hall.

Audiovisual hall from the temporary exhibition gallery.

The shop has space on the floor below which is shown linked by a staircase as a possible additional selling area or alternatively as storage space. The cloakroom and shop are arranged so that they face visitors as they descend the stairs, or leave other parts of the building.

From the entrance hall can also be seen the way in to the temporary exhibition gallery, the lifts to the other floors and the stairs down to the lecture hall foyer. These lead off the part of the hallway to the north of the circular space. Here there are benches to wait, out of the main bustle, telephones and a lavatory for the disabled. The public may also view presentations in the audiovisual hall below through a glass screen that may be folded back depending on the sound level acceptable in that part of the foyer.

The floor of the temporary exhibition space is 2.5m (8ft) lower than the entrance hall and is entered down a circular flight of stairs, the centre circle forming a landing. The lifts are adjacent so that visitors arrive at the same place for an entry desk to the exhibitions. The lower floor level gives a 5m high space with a 1m deep ceiling void for lighting and air conditioning services. The total area is 720m², near the maximum required by the brief, but has only four columns giving substantial flexibility of arrangement. A detailed design of the space has not been made as the requirements of the Gallery must be further defined for a useful contribution to be made. However, it is our opinion that many galleries of this nature have unnecessary screen systems on a rigid grid designed for them which are subsequently ignored by the designers of the temporary exhibitions, who prefer the freedom to erect walls of all shapes and sizes to suit the particular show.

The back of the audiovisual auditorium is at the same level as the gallery floor, so that it may easily be incorporated into the sequence of an exhibition or entered at the end on the way out, its exit being via the same stairs and lift doors as the gallery. It can also be used separately while a show is being mounted. The picture store and packing are adjacent to the gallery and both lead directly to the loading bay picture lift.

The loading bay is also positioned conveniently for the bookshop and its stores and hoist. Externally this position is unobtrusive from the major approaches to the Gallery from Pall Mall East and down St Martin's Street from Leicester Square.

First Floor Plan.

Lower Floor Plan.

Gallery Floor Plan.

Attic Floor Plan.

Ground-floor plan.

CAMPBELL ZOGOLOVITCH WILKINSON & GOUGH

## Lower floors

The lecture hall foyer is approached by its own grand curving staircase and is an echo of the circular hall above. It is large enough to cope, should one audience's arrival overlap with another's departure. In the foyer is the other counter of the cloakroom system, a bar, and a large number of lavatories. A green room can be entered from the foyer and the stage. The auditorium itself seats 294 and can be opened up by a vertical sliding sound-proof wall to incorporate the audiovisual area as well, making 500 seats in all. The seats are on a shallow rake and uphol-stered more in the manner of a theatre than a lecture hall. Many lecturers today use a range of aids and few use anything less than two slide projectors; these would be housed in a control console at the rear of the auditorium and be controllable from the platform, which is wide and deep to accommodate numbers of speakers and allow them to look at the screen without falling off stage.

On the service side at this lowest level are the gallery workshops, further book-stores, the plant room supplying air con-ditioning to the non-gallery floors through separate systems coinciding with the different time and use requirements of the parts of the building. (Fresh air is taken from the existing lightwell on the west end of the gallery, this being the point furthest from traffic fumes.) A car park is accessed by a car lift from the semicircular tower in St Martin's Street. This lift would also be used for the servic-ing and replacement of transformers, generators and other plant.

There are various possibilities of more or less tortuous links back to the main building from this lower level which could be further discussed.

## First floor

From the entrance hall on the ground floor, the principal staircase curves up to the first floor. From that landing the stairs on up to the galleries are directly ahead. To one side of that flight is the

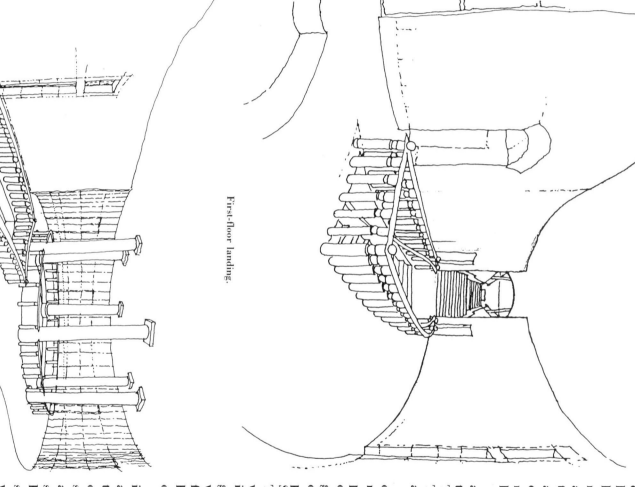

First-floor landing.

View towards restaurant.

entrance to the information room via a light lobby. The lifts open on to this landing area. Off to one side are the other main lavatories of the extension, as close as possible to the picture galleries without taking space on that floor. Behind the ascending visitor and therefore ahead on descent is the restaurant. It is app-roached by the balcony around the double-height opening of the entrance hall.

There is also a link bridge at this level across to the end of the passage containing the offices of the Director and keepers. This would be for the use of senior staff, Trustees and others visiting the extension and its boardroom suite.

The restaurant itself would seat 200 comfortably. It is self-service with sepa-rate meal and snack counters as in the present facility. The room enjoys specta-cular views over the Square with a mainly glass curved wall and also over the stair-case and foyer space through a glass partition, the closer views into Whitcomb Street being through separate windows. The southwest corner has an open turret with its perforated stone openings allow-ing views down Pall Mall East (whilst giving security protection to a height that would otherwise be too easily reached from the street). The restaurant may also be approached externally from the porti-co staircase down from the gallery floor.

The kitchen with its ancillary stores is in the service area in the centre of the plan and is supplied by the service hoist from the loading bay. The publications offices occupy the whole of the north side in a U-shape to give it maximum window area and space of average 8m (26ft) depth. The staff share lavatories, changing areas and locker space with the warders who have a separate rest room with windows on the west side.

## Attic floor

The top floor is approached by the lifts or a staircase from the gallery-floor level. A bridge leads to the vestibule which has a circular opening down to the gallery be-low, and a similar rooflight dome above.

The boardroom, dining room and balcony are enfiladed and served by a kitchen with a hoist and stair on the west side. The boardroom has both a clerestory light for viewing paintings and side windows for normal light and view, which would be shuttered to provide walls for presentations. To the north of the vestibule are a divisible committee room and a north light studio for the use of the artist in residence.

## Gallery floor

The top flight of the main staircase from the first-floor level to the galleries floor arrives in the same space as the bridge link from the existing galleries. Neither of these spaces is intended for picture hanging, so they may have windows for views and side lighting as well as a lantern over the cross-axis. The level of light will be subdued to prepare for entering the first gallery but rays of sunlight can be allowed to penetrate. This space would provide seating, gallery guides and further information. It would be a reorientation point for visitors from both halves of the building.

The first gallery is straight ahead at the top of the stairs and there is also a separate entry into the special Gallery 17 described below. Gallery 1 is the only gallery not to open directly off, or be part of, the main axis, and acts as a prelude to it. This first room must at once be intimate, to enhance the works, but physically large in order to accommodate the inevitable crowding that occurs in the first room of any arrangement. The room is square with two side niches on one wall. The walls, which are of Bath stone, are 4m (13ft) high rising in a semicircular arch on the north wall on which to hang the Segna Crucifix. The ceiling is in the form of a square of intersecting plastered arch vaults supporting clerestory windows. The centre is supported by a single column, articulating the room into more intimate spaces.

There are two door openings, one each to Galleries 2 and 2A. The former allows a view of an axis through to Galleries 3 and

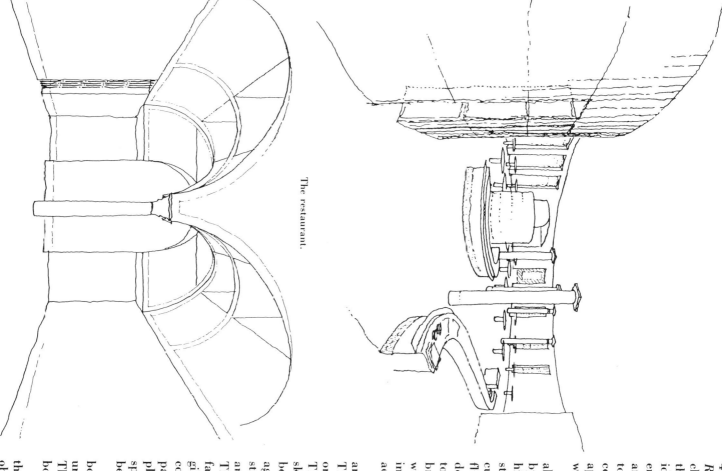

The restaurant.

Gallery 1.

4 terminating in the Uccello *Battle of San Romano*. However, this one might be kept closed by an iron railing gate to represent the hiatus caused to the progress of the ideas of Duccio. The visitor would next enter Gallery 2A with the Wilton diptych and the altarpieces of Group 2, which are too small to be seen with their large counterparts. This would make the approach to Gallery 2 through the long wall opposite the Orcagna altarpiece.

Gallery 2 follows a pattern common to all the Italian galleries; a room 7m (23ft) by 11m (36ft) with side walls 6m (20ft) high supporting five semicircular arched stone ribs making four bays. The walls curve in between the arches in panels flush with the face of the arch. The windows stand vertically on a stone band on top of the panels. The windows are brought slightly in from the plane of the wall so that they can be lower than those in the main axis gallery, which must run across above them.

The ceiling between the ribs is coffered, and matches that in the main Gallery. There is a large semicircular opening high on the west wall into the central gallery. This element and other details such as skirting, door surrounds and ribs are to be of Bath stone, which gives protection against damage at vulnerable points. The stone would also be used to make plinths and projections to support altarpieces. The walls of this particular space with its fabulous altarpieces are proposed to be gilded. The leaf would be unburnished in contrast to the burnished frames of the paintings. Gold is most beautiful when placed on a background of more gold. The space, and particularly the light, would be absolutely ravishing.

The floors throughout are to be oak boards. (Stone and ceramics seem unnatural on an upper floor, carpet unsuitable.) The scale of the spaces demands wide boards and the colour should be mellow.

Many different methods of protecting the paintings from public touch have been observed. Most constitute a formal reminder rather than prevention. We prefer

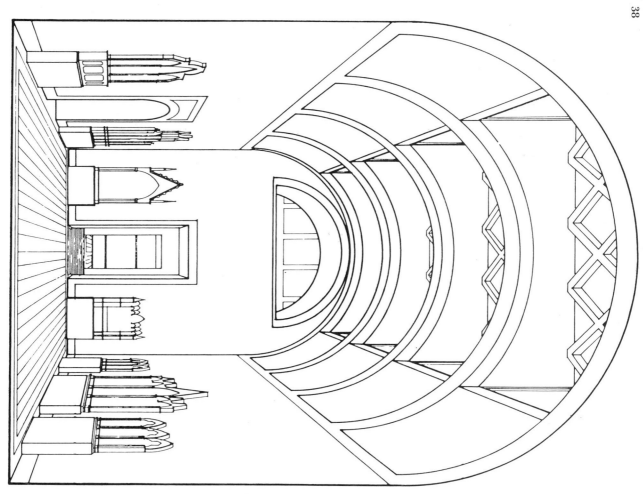

Gallery 2.

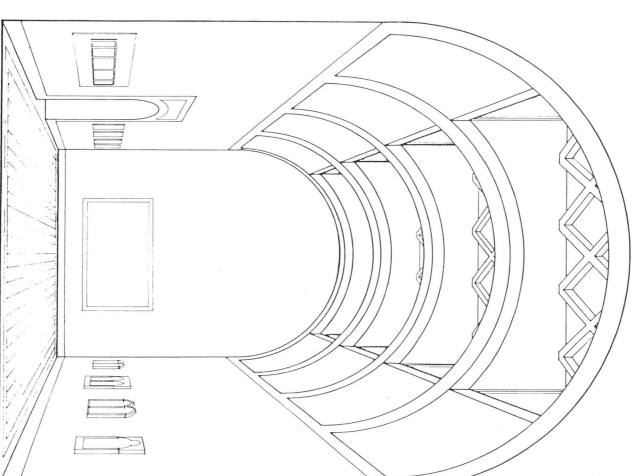

Gallery 4.

the prosaic rope to other more rigid and tensioned types. But the vertical supports should be firmly anchored and upright, so they remain ordered and upright.

Gallery 3 is at the north end of the main axis gallery, which may now be described. The space is 8m (26ft) wide and 15m (50ft) high. Clerestory windows run the full length of the space. The lower 7m (23ft) of the walls are of Bath stone. Natural materials make the most beautiful backgrounds for pictures and this particular stone with its mellowness and warm colour would be eminently suited to the paintings. Internally, Bath stone can be detailed to be very closely jointed and spun-sanded afterwards. The effect would be a smooth, even finish, whilst retaining the intrinsic patina and depth of grain. The cross-walls dividing the groups would also be of stone up to its top height with arched openings in their centre.

Above the stone, at a level that would be called the triforium in a church, are semicircular openings in the walls. Some are deep niches, and some open into the upper volume of the side galleries as has been seen in Gallery 2. This makes an additional spatial link between galleries that should be quite thrilling. The windows themselves are divided by piers (to prevent angled daylight causing problems at a distance down the gallery). This allows space for a small access walkway in the depth of the wall for maintenance of the windows.

The high windows have a number of advantages. The light is more easily controlled by simple mechanical methods (the sun's path falls within a moderate cone). The light falls on the opposite wall and not on the floor, and can be simply organised to fall on the desired part of the wall. Vertical windows have far fewer problems of maintenance and cleaning as they do not collect dirt and pigeon droppings so readily.

The intention is that the daylight be perceived by the visitor as natural, so that it will be allowed to fluctuate within prescribed safe limits with time of day and

Gallery 3.

conditions outside. It is intended that a high percentage of hours should be daylit alone since this is the optimum light for the pictures and the purpose of the Gallery. Artificial lighting to balance the overall level will be introduced in a number of steps that respond to general outside conditions.

The detailed design requires models, mockups and extensive testing to finalise the best type of control system for this configuration (which can be considered as a type of clerestory light). We are assured at this stage by those we have consulted that the daylighting source is of the correct order and scale and that our strategy can lead to an arrangement that is relatively simple to operate and maintain, for, apart from the considerations of the beauty of unhomogenised light, we would wish to avoid offering the panacea of a computer-controlled arrangement, since systems tend to have problems in proportion to their complexity.

The intention is that the artificial lighting will not imitate daylight. It will be perceived by the visitor as different, in the way one would expect when visiting a gallery after nightfall or at dusk. There will be no need for so-called daylight fluorescents with their totally false sense of colour verity, for they do not just make a cold, unpleasant atmosphere, but have a dangerously uneven spectral emission with troughs and peaks (mostly in the blue end of the spectrum) that the eye cannot make adjustment for. Tungsten and halogen sources also have an unequal spectral distribution, but it is evenly biased, and the eye can know to make some allowance for this; moreover, being stronger at the warm end, it gives a pleasant overall environment.

The lighting is contained in the coffered ceiling and accessed from a space above it. The lights will be organised to give around 150-200 lux on the pictures and slightly less on the walls around them. The appearance of the ceiling will be of a lapiz blue punctuated by many stars. Being 15m high, this decorative feature will not clash or be seen when viewing the

CAMPBELL ZOGOLOVITCH WILKINSON & GOUGH

pictures. The only problem with lighting from above a ceiling is that it remains in darkness. So to light it and provide an apparent general light source, there are a number of chandeliers (no other word for it). These are rather austere, of concentric steel hoops holding plain fittings with upward reflectors. Their height and position ensure that they will not be a source of reflections.

Gallery 3 itself is quite small and contains the Lorenzo Monaco altarpiece which is on the north end wall of the space. The Gentile loan and the Austrian Trinity flank the opening to the long space.

Gallery 4, International Gothicising, continues the first axis across the north end culminating in the Uccello mentioned earlier. One long wall is devoted to the wonderful Sassetta St Francis series. The Angelico Predella is mounted on a stone backing panel flush with wall surface which in these other galleries is to be Venetian stucco. This is a marvellous type of plaster that can be made coloured, being integral it is not flat and homogeneous like paint but has the depth of a natural material. There are various methods of application of the coloured part itself to give either a relatively even or a watery or other effects to it. The finished stucco is waxed and can be made to appear matt or polished up by degrees to a marble-like sheen. This room would be a soft terracotta.

Gallery 5 is the first of the Northern galleries, which are of a smaller scale than the others. The plan is 7m (23ft) by 9m (29ft), surmounted by a shallow square segmented dome in the Soane/Lutyens manner, carrying a central lantern for daylight windows with a coffered ceiling providing artificial light as described before.

The walls are also of stucco with Bath stone details. The stucco of this room would be a light grey putty colour to complement the pictures. Van Eyck's *Marriage* hangs centrally flanked by his two other portraits and those of Campin's turbaned man and almond-eyed lady.

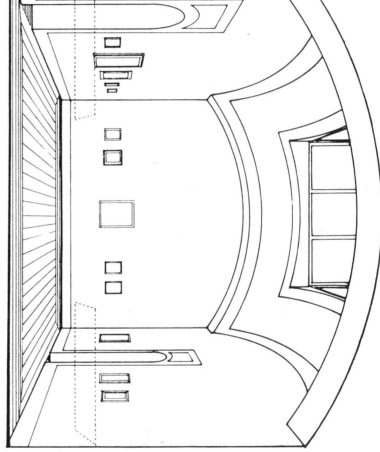

Gallery 5.

The Madonna of the firescreen is adjacent to them. The Weydens are together on the other wall. The cased pictures are under the arch on the east side.

Group 6 of Masaccio and the Early Florentines continues in the central gallery. Again not a large space, the expectation of the whole vista is still held back. The Lippis flank the opening through to Gallery 7 where the whole volume is revealed and continues with the central works of the period: early Bellini, Mantegna and Antonello.

The transition to Group 8 is defined by niches in the wall. The major painting is Piero's altarpiece which stands in the centre of the space (back-to-back with an altarpiece of Group 16). The Prado has an example of this 'hang' which is marvellous, but Piero may need a backing wall to prevent distraction from behind. The Pieros and the Joos are on either side wall.

Gallery 9 is the second Northern room. The Memlinc triptych stands on a projecting stone plinth on the west wall with Bouts to one side and other works by Memlinc opposite. The walls could be a slightly greener grey than Gallery 5 to enhance the pastoral nature of the works.

The Northern side is continued in Group 10, works from Cologne and Westphalia. These wholly religious pictures would look excellent on a watery black background. The colour of Venetian stucco can be made pale without becoming pastel. *The Master of the Life of the Virgin* panels would be freestanding across the direction of entry, while *The Master of Liesborn* works would be grouped at the west end of the room, the pairs hanging on adjacent walls across a corner to enhance their strong architectural spaces.

Gallery 11 is across the central space and houses the works of Crivelli and Ferrara. This large group needs a five-

bay version of the Italian pattern room. It will be dominated by the extraordinary Demidoff altarpiece but there are a number of other important large Crivellis, strange Turas and the delightful Costa concert party. A colour to suit them all is difficult, but some soft greens would be interesting to experiment with.

The Botticelli room is Gallery 12. The variation in this space is the further framing of the walls with stone pilasters running up the corners of the room to increase their definition. *Venus and Mars* would be on one end wall and the *Tondo Adoration* would have architectural resonance on the other, with the *Mystic Nativity* in the centre of a side wall.

Later Florentine and Umbrian works occupy the south end of the main axis gallery. The Pollaiuolo St Sebastian altarpiece stands centrally in the same way as the Piero. The south end wall might be either the Botticini on a high plinth or possibly the Filippino Lippi. There is the space to differentiate the frescos which can be set in a shallow plastered niche.

Gallery 14 is the last Italian side gallery. Mantegna's altarpiece would face the entrance on the end wall, either side being dominated by his and Bellini's paintings. A pale azure blue would make a slightly ethereal background to the grisaille group and complement the beautiful Bellinis.

The equivalent later Netherlandish works are across the central axis in Gallery 15, a variation on the Northern space. It has two very different sized triptyches which gave rise to the idea of a small octagonal niche off a larger octagonal space, the open doors echoing the angles of the room. These richer works would be enhanced by a quite strong amber background, the colour in the frame around the exquisite Geertgen *Nativity*.

The altarpieces of Group 16 define a central space of the long gallery and denote the secondary axis entrances to side galleries and the other minor circulation route to the stairs. These largest of all

works will be seen at their best in the middle of this tremendous space.

The Gallery's brief suggests that Gallery 17 be for portraits. We prefer to extend the idea so that all paintings have a place with their historical groups. But any may be brought to this gallery temporarily to make other connections of type or influence. Also the gallery could be used for the display of new acquisitions, loans, etc. This gallery, with its possibility of special use, is positioned adjacent to the arrival space at the top of the stairs, where it can be entered separately or closed off without affecting the visitors to the other spaces.

Between the side galleries are further smaller spaces; they are not daylit and do not have paintings in them. They are intended as galleries providing additional material about the works in the collection to put them in a further context or make connections with works in other galleries. It is important that these spaces do not interfere visually with the main galleries. They are arranged so that when their doors are open, they form a baffle such that they cannot be seen into from the other spaces.

Above these intermediate rooms are the air-handling systems for the galleries. A number of localised units make individual gallery control possible. They reduce standby capacity and require only short duct runs. The only visible outlets in the galleries will be from five of the smaller semicircular features in the large semicircular blind openings of the triforium in the central gallery and from above one door on each of the side galleries. The inlets are hidden in the connecting spaces between these galleries.

The total hanging length of the galleries is 505m.

The curved return loggia is of Portland stone with full-height fluted glass through which to enjoy the view.

Campbell Zogolovitch Wilkinson & Gough — Architects
Alan Baxter & Associates — Structural Engineers
YRM Engineers — Mechanical Engineers
Claude Engle — Lighting Consultant
Andrews & Boyd — Quantity Surveyors

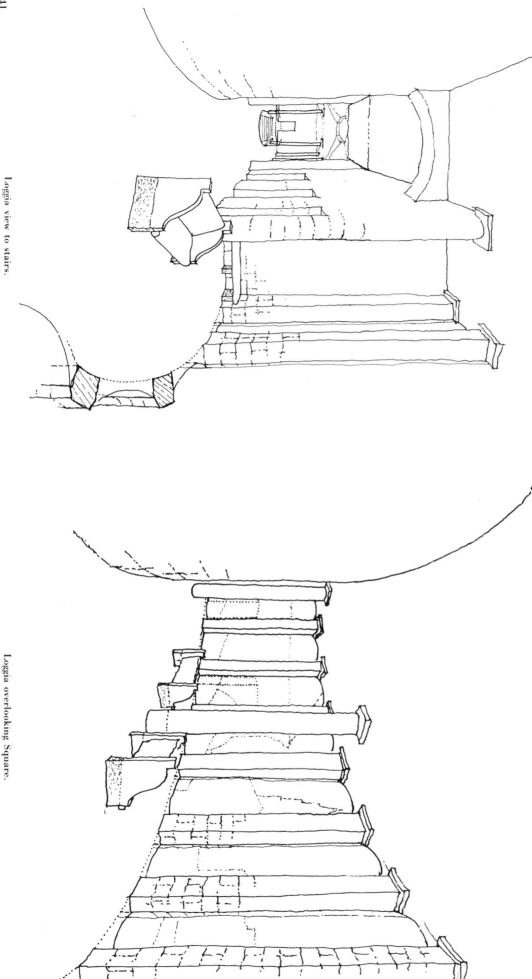

Loggia view to stairs.

Loggia overlooking Square.

**CAMPBELL ZOGOLOVITCH WILKINSON & GOUGH**

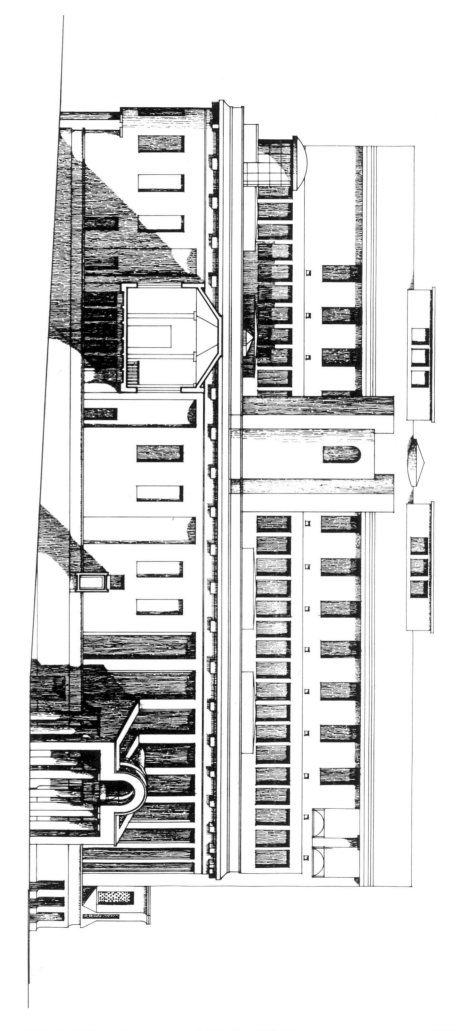

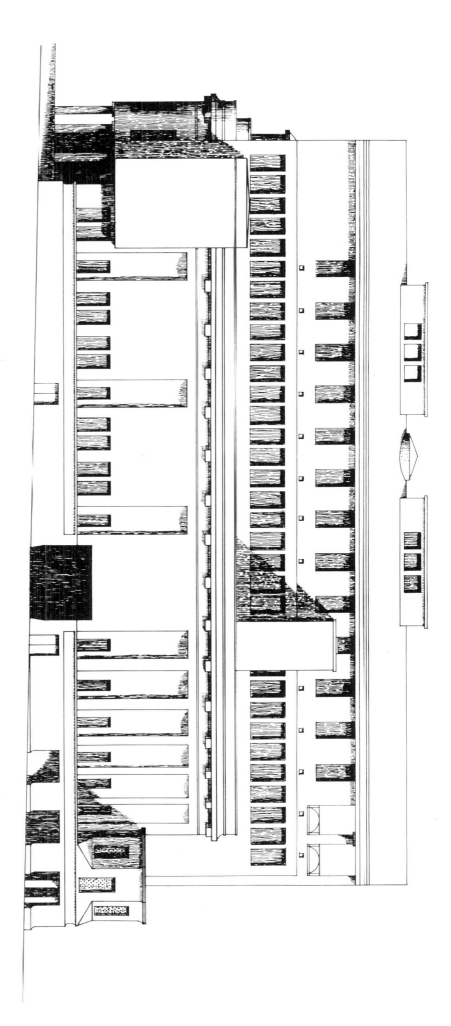

West elevation.

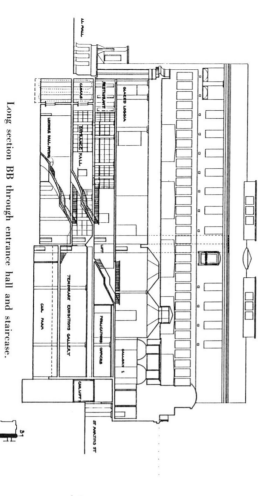

Long section BB through entrance hall and staircase.

National Gallery · Hampton Site Extension Sections.

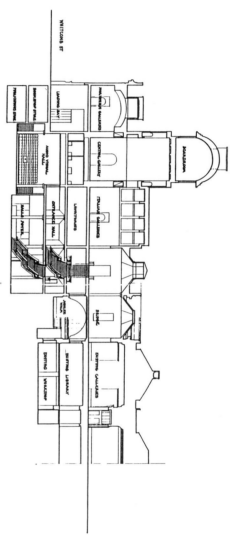

Cross-section AA through galleries and bridge.

Long section CC through central gallery and auditoria.

Campbell Zogolovitch Wilkinson & Gough January 1986.

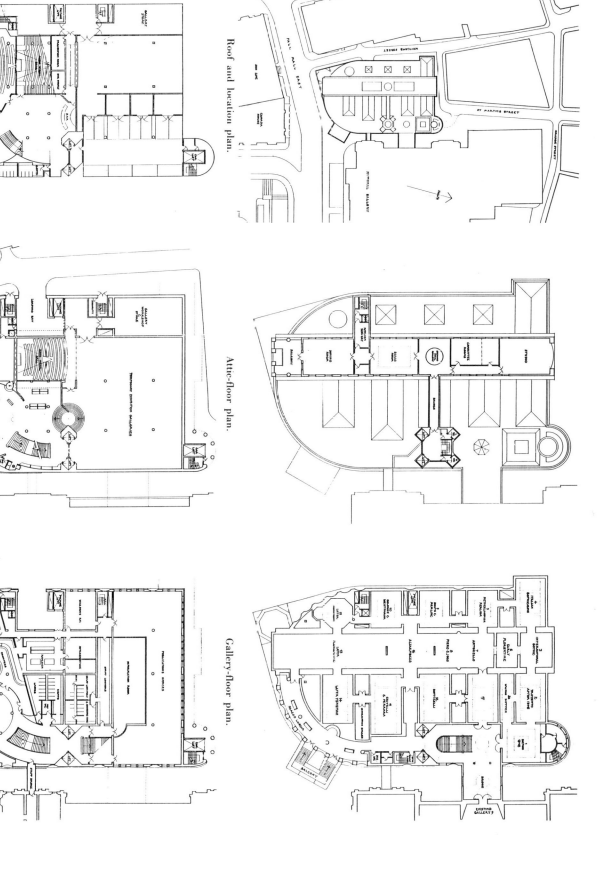

Roof and location plan.

Attic-floor plan.

Gallery-floor plan.

Lower-floor plans.

National Gallery · Hampton Site Extension Plans.

Ground-floor plan.

Campbell Zogolovitch Wilkinson & Gough January 1986.

First-floor plan.

CAMPBELL ZOGOLOVITCH WILKINSON & GOUGH ·

# Henry Nichols Cobb of I M Pei & Partners

**Foreword**

The drawings and models documenting my preliminary design study are essentially self-explanatory. Nonetheless, I want to avail myself of this opportunity to discuss briefly some of the principal concerns and intentions that have motivated my design. In doing so I shall not attempt to give a comprehensive description of the scheme. Rather, I shall assume that the reader has had access to my drawings and, preferably, has them at hand while perusing this report.

**Exterior form and expression**

In shaping a building volume for the Hampton site extension, I have remained faithful to the tentative conclusions drawn from my initial site analysis as presented to the committee last September. Principal among these was the observation that a curved building face derived from a rotational geometry constitutes the most appropriate response to the site's complex urban setting at the intersection of Pall Mall and Trafalgar Square. This proposition has now been given specific form as a semicircular screen-wall articulating the most prominent corner of a building volume that otherwise simply fills the available land area (as indeed it must if it is to provide the required accommodation). This curved screen-wall, by virtue of its position, its shape and its ornament, is the indisputable architectural cynosure of the new building. Standing as it does at an extraordinary 'pressure point' of London's public realm, the screen-wall is the natural vehicle for deployment of an architectural apparatus composed of

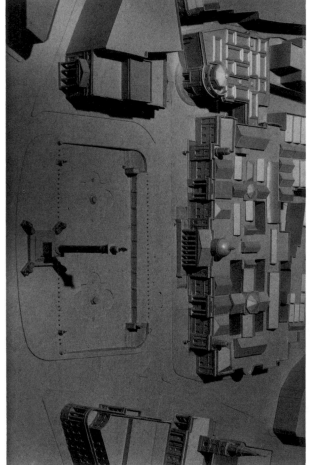

Photo Nathaniel Lieberman

Model: aerial view.

classical elements and intended to communicate in a quite precise way the institutional role of the new building as not merely an extension but a significant augmentation of the National Gallery.

The fulfilment of this intent requires a design strategy that shows appropriate deference to the main building by acknowledging its best features while at the same time compensating for some of its salient weaknesses. Among the latter, the most disturbing to me is the misleading impression conveyed by the Trafalgar Square facade with respect to the hierarchy of space that lies behind it. The internal primacy of the exhibition galleries is nowhere evidenced; indeed, it is contradicted by a fenestration scheme that gives the ground-floor offices the

status of a 'noble floor', while the main gallery level above has the appearance of a secondary upper floor of a vastly overextended country house. Only the blindness of this upper range of windows hints, rather ineffectively, that something else might be afoot.

Fortunately, however, this confusing and unsatisfactory two-storey array is overlaid with a colossal Corinthian order, giving the facade both a distinctive character and an appropriately public scale. Clearly this order, with its well-defined entablature and base, is the strongest unifying feature of Wilkins' facade and constitutes the one element (other than Portland stone) that the new building unquestionably needs to have in common with the old if both are to be perceived as

belonging to a single institution. In considering how best to introduce this colossal order into my design, I experimented first with columns, both engaged and free-standing, but found through models that they inevitably challenged the primacy of the existing central portico — a primacy that I firmly believe should be maintained. The less assertive and actually more characteristic pilaster therefore recommended itself, and the decision to employ this motif then laid the foundation for all subsequent steps in the design.

Adoption of the colossal order of the main building as the governing element in the facade of the extension brought me immediately face to face with the problem of entry: as it happens, the base of the colossal order is too high to be easily accessible from street level and too low to allow for a gracious entry beneath it. While wrestling with this difficulty, and being preoccupied also with the importance of establishing the gallery level as unequivocally the 'noble floor', of the new building, it dawned on me that both problems could be solved by introducing a smaller order of columns below but overlapping the colossal one — a strategy invented by Michelangelo for the facade of the Conservators' Palace on the Capitoline in Rome. The particular merit of this strategy as I have interpreted it here is that it dramatises the poignant duality of intention inherent in this building: on the one hand, as a major public institution located in the heart of a capital city, the building ought to invite entry and play an active, engaging role on the urban stage; on the other hand, as the repository of paintings whose significance surely trans-

Model: Pall Mall East view.

Model: view from Trafalgar Square.

HENRY N COBB OF I M PEI & PARTNERS

cends that of even the greatest symbols of national identity, the building ought to maintain a certain 'distance' between the place of contemplation within and the distracting busyness that flows constantly around it. My aim has been to find a way of communicating this duality while striking a delicate balance between deference and self-assertion in the relationship of the new building to the old.

In pursuit of this goal, I found that the curved screen-wall by itself, though successful in its engagement with the street, was insufficient: the second half of the duality of intention that I sought to convey could be expressed only by creating an explicit awareness of a space within – a chamber having an autonomous value quite independent of the external circumstances of its urban setting. This discovery led me to explore the possibility of allowing a dome to rise from a circular drum behind the screen-wall. But once again I found through modelling that this

feature would pose an unacceptable threat to the primacy of the central dome of the main building. The solution that finally emerged from this search – an octagonal cupola of low profile rising behind the pierced attic of the screen-wall – has two advantages: first, it takes its place comfortably and with dignity, but also with appropriate understatement, among the several landmarks ornamenting the periphery of Trafalgar Square; and second, it presents a profile and roof form specifically evocative of the early Renaissance in Italy.

In shaping the building envelope beyond the limits of the curved screen-wall, I have been motivated by concern for several specific circumstances of the urban context. To the west, the building face has been placed parallel to Pall Mall but set back some 6m from the property line in order to permit the curved screen-wall and its entry portico to be seen by those approaching from the west on Pall

Mall. In the widened footpath thus created, I have placed a pair of stanchions supporting a banner whose high visibility from Trafalgar Square makes it the ideal locus for announcing special exhibitions taking place within the new extension. At the other end of the curved screen-wall, where it engages Jubilee Walk, a more complex strategy is called for, in response to the proximity of the main building. Here I have proposed a matching pavilion framing a gateway into Jubilee Walk, and in the base of this pavilion I have placed an entry at grade level, allowing direct access to the lecture theatre as well as convenient access for the handicapped.

My intention in the treatment of the bridge link over Jubilee Walk has been to transform it from a mere overpass into a columned pavilion offering an attractive architectural event in the passage from Trafalgar Square to Leicester Square.

Here I have employed the same Tuscan order that frames each of the openings in the main entry portico. In both instances, the chunky sturdiness of this order is appropriate to its role in supporting the massive unfenestrated volume of the permanent exhibition galleries above.

As I mentioned at the outset, with the exception of the Pall Mall frontage the new extension fills the available land area, and the building envelope is treated with utmost simplicity: plain channelled walling – a Soanian device – is stretched between entablature and base, both of which features conform in profile to the corresponding elements of the main building. The only exceptional events in this envelope are an array of windows opening into the restaurant and bookstore on the Jubilee Walk side, and a projecting feature on the Whitcomb Street face acknowledging the termination of the great east/west axis that extends the entire length of the National Gallery.

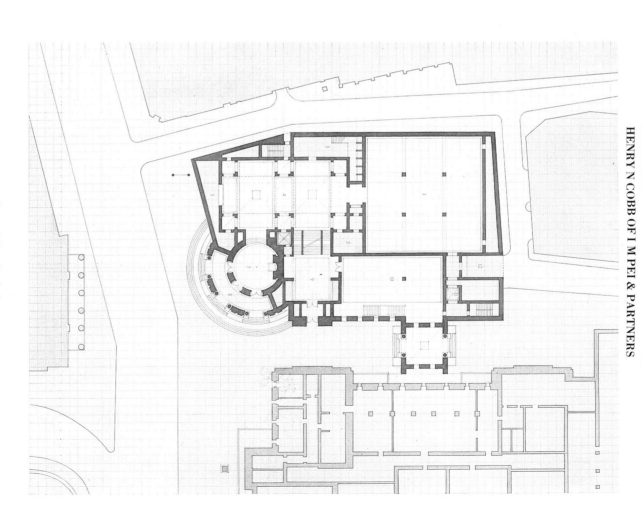

HENRY N COBB OF I M PEI & PARTNERS

Basement-level plan.

| | |
|---|---|
| 1 | Lecture theatre |
| 2 | Projection booth |
| 3 | Box office |
| 4 | Lobby |
| 5 | Cloakroom |
| 6 | Public toilets |
| 7 | Passenger lift |
| 8 | Audiovisual room |
| 9 | Publications department shop |
| 10 | Publications department goods-in area |
| 11 | Goods lift |
| 12 | Warders' accommodation |

Ground-floor level plan.

| | |
|---|---|
| 1 | Temporary exhibition gallery |
| 2 | Office |
| 3 | Information room |
| 4 | Entrance lobby |
| 5 | Cloakroom |
| 6 | Passenger lift |
| 7 | Vestibule (level 13,19) |
| 8 | Porch |
| 9 | Grade-level entrance |
| 10 | Publications department shop (upper level) |
| 11 | Goods lift |
| 12 | Service entrance |

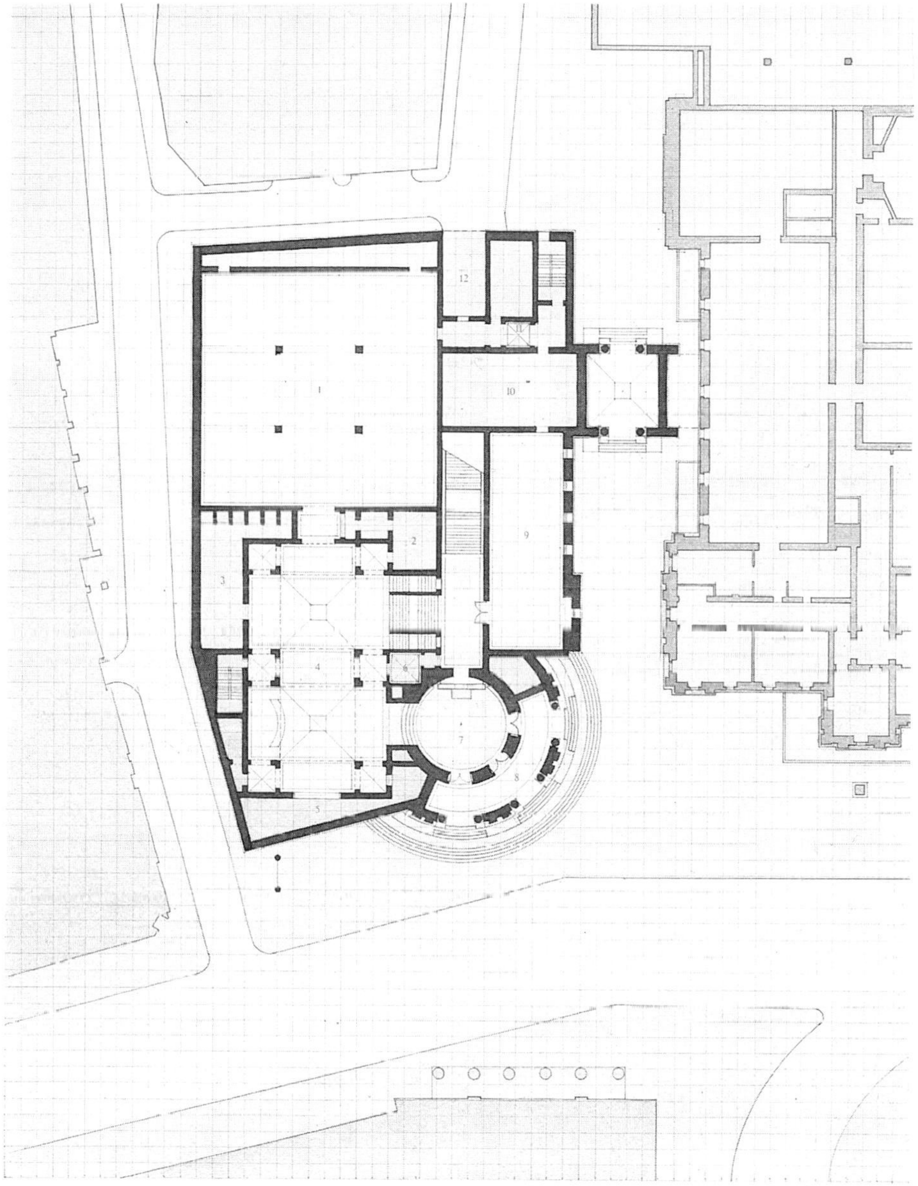

49

First-floor level plan.

1 Temporary exhibition gallery
2 Office
3 Information room
4 Entrance lobby
5 Cloakroom
6 Passenger lift
7 Vestibule
8 Porch
9 Restaurant (level 15.76)
10 Kitchen
11 Goods lift
12 Service entrance

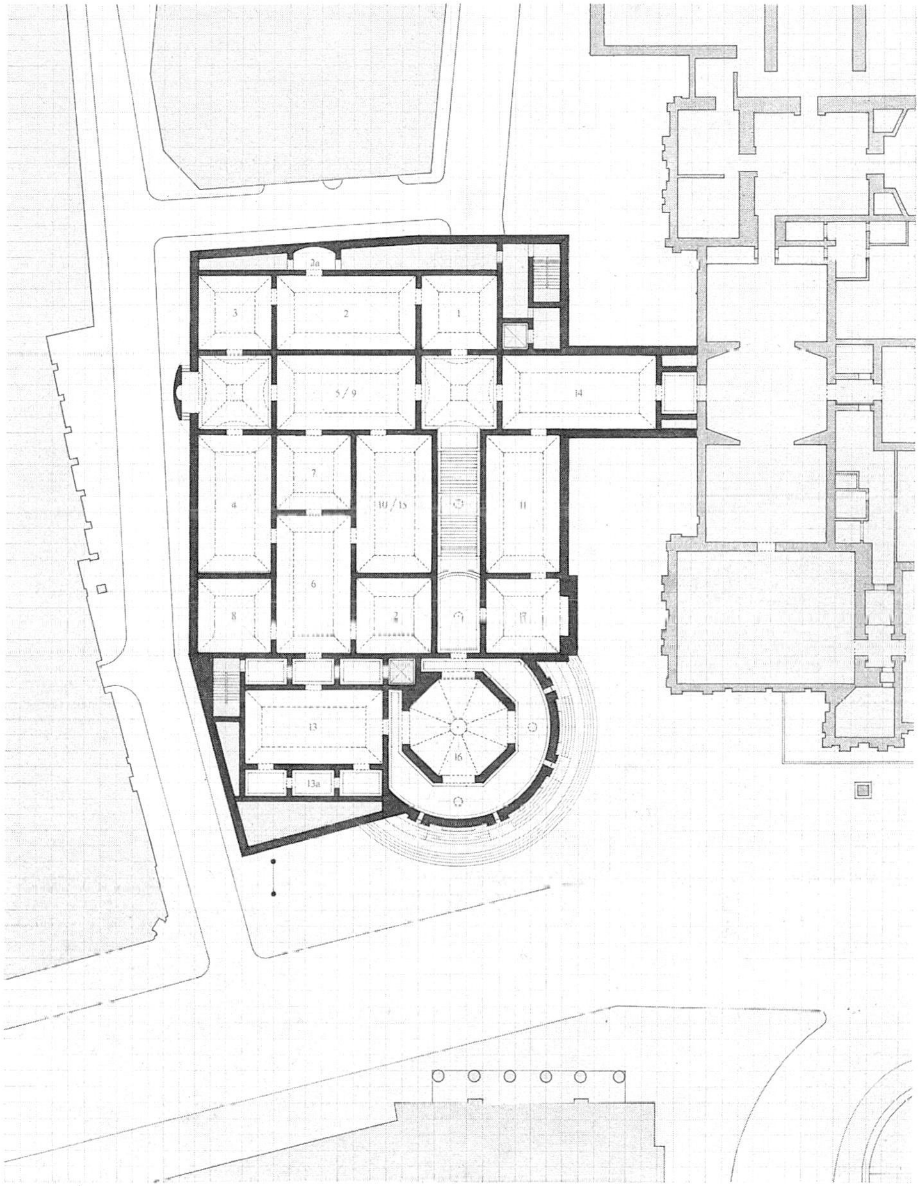

Gallery-level plan.

1 Duecento & Trecento to 1348
2 Trecento after 1348
2a Wilton diptych
3 International Gothic
4 Italian Gothicising
5 Netherlandish Realism
6 Early Florentine
7 Antonello, Early Mantegna, Bellini
8 Piero della Francesca & Joos
9 Bouts & Memlinc
10 Cologne & Westphalia
11 Crivelli & Ferrara
12 Botticelli
13 Later Florentine, etc
13a Didactic gallery (drawings, etc)
14 Later Venetian
15 Later Northern
16 Altarpieces
17 Portraits

HENRY N COBB OF I M PEI & PARTNERS

## Entry sequence

An 8m vertical distance between street and gallery levels might seem to constitute a serious inconvenience to museum-goers. But in this case at least, it has a compensating advantage, in as much as it mandates an extended entry sequence and hence offers the opportunity to shape the visitor's experience in such a way as to enhance appreciation of the paintings which are encountered at the end of the journey.

A key objective in structuring the entry sequence in my design has been to conceal the fact that one is climbing two whole storeys in order to reach one's destination. This has been accomplished by dividing the ascent into a series of relatively easy stages, each of which plays a distinct role in the gradual transition from the realm of the city to the realm of art. This transition begins out of doors at street level with a broad curved flight of steps leading up to the sheltered portico, the floor of which is 1½m above the footpath – just high enough to place visitors securely above the turmoil of the street and permit them to command a splendid view into Trafalgar Square. Each of the three openings in this portico addresses one of the three principal features of its surroundings: Pall Mall, Trafalgar Square and the main building of the National Gallery. Passing through the portico, visitors next enter a circular vestibule that serves as a mediating space between outside and inside. Within this shallow-domed room, with its walls clad in Portland stone to match the exterior, a basin of water with a splashing fountain is placed to one side, masking the harsh sounds of the city with its gentle music.

From the vestibule a single large opening leads up a few more steps to the entrance lobby. This generously proportioned rectangular gathering place, with the main cloakroom to one side, gives access to all destinations within the building, but most importantly to the broad staircase leading up by easy 2m stages to the permanent exhibition galleries. During the latter stages of this ascent, as shown in the section looking west, this staircase takes the form of a vaulted hall rising straight through the gallery level and illuminated by three small skylights that dramatise the verticality of the space without allowing too much light to enter. Indeed, the control of light is in my view

as important as the shaping of space in the entry sequence, as it is my intention that despite the relatively low level of illumination to be maintained in the exhibition galleries, visitors arriving there should feel that these rooms are expansive and brightly lit in comparison with the spaces through which they have passed. The

extended passage from street to galleries affords a needed opportunity to adjust the museum-goer's eyes gradually to darkness so that the arrival in Gallery 1, with the Segna di Bonaventura Crucifix high on the wall opposite the staircase, is felt as a moment of intense visual and spiritual enchantment.

**Permanent exhibition galleries**
We have come now to the heart of the enterprise. My discussion of the permanent exhibition galleries will be presented under four headings: Gallery configuration, Lighting, Gallery Sequence, Cupola gallery.

*Gallery configuration:* As those members of the committee who visited Portland will recall, I have long harboured a strong bias against flat translucent ceiling planes in museum galleries and equally a bias in favour of opaque sloping ceiling surfaces that reflect daylight entering from above. However, in approaching this gallery design problem I put aside my earlier bias and examined the whole range of possibilities without prejudice. Hence my present proposal to pursue what I call the domed clerestory configuration in this building is not simply a carryover from the Portland Museum but rather the result of a thorough reconsideration of all available options.

My reason for returning to the domed clerestory form of gallery is simply that in my judgment this configuration offers the best antidote to the deadening effect on the gallery space (and hence on the visitor's experience) which inevitably results from satisfying the requirement that all wall surfaces receive approximately the same amount of light at the hanging level. (In order to provide 500m of hanging length on one floor in this building, it will clearly be necessary to hang pictures on all four walls of most gallery spaces, thus precluding the possibility of light coming from one side only.) In these circumstances I believe it is beneficial to minimise the viewer's awareness of a horizontal ceiling plane, and this is best accom-

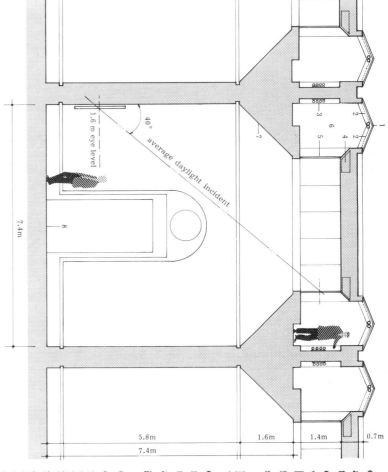

7.4m

1.6 m eye level

40°

average daylight incident

8

7.4m

5.8m   1.6m   1.4m   0.7m

LEGEND

1. Translucent white skylight with UV filtering
2. Sensor-controlled motor-operated opaque roller shade
3. Recessed supplemental fluorescent lighting (4000° Kelvin)
4. Accessible compartment for recessed incandescent focal light fixtures to be installed if and as required to supplement general illumination
5. Patterned diffusing translucent glass
6. Cavity surfaces painted matte white - highest reflectance
7. High reflectance surfaces painted white or off-white - 80%
8. Floor reflectance - 20 to 40%

Typical gallery section: lighting proposal.

plished by sloping the ceiling upwards from the four walls to a central opening enclosed by a clerestory rising vertically above. This strategy proves to work best when at least one horizontal dimension of the gallery is about equal to the height of the room from the floor to the bottom of the clerestory', and this accounts for my adoption of a 7.4m or 13.8m width for all galleries, with the other dimension being either 7.4m or 13.8m, thus producing two distinct gallery shapes, one square and one rectangular.

Here I should make it clear that I do not insist on limiting the gallery shapes to only two. On the other hand, at this stage I have not found any compelling reason – with the obvious exception of Group 16 – why there should be more variety in the gallery sequence than these two can provide. Furthermore, because of the number of separate groupings called for in the provisional brief (the 'Ideal Hang'), I think it is arguable that the interplay of two gallery shapes is more satisfying and less distracting to the visitor than a greater variety. I believe these two shapes provide ample opportunity for a number of different hanging schemes in each and that the resulting balance of diverse hanging arrangements within two clearly identifiable and well-proportioned spatial configurations is likely to produce experiential conditions most favourable to appreciation of the paintings. But having said this I must acknowledge that in the ease of a permanent collection of the highest quality such as this one, any generalised principles of gallery design should be considered tentative until they have been tested, room by room and picture by picture – a process that has scarcely been possible in the circumstances of this preliminary design study. What I am offering here is my best judgment based on my general knowledge of the collection and my understanding of the curatorial intentions of the Gallery staff.

*Lighting:* Although there is nothing especially novel about the domed clerestory configuration that I propose for the exhibi-

tion galleries – it was Soane's preferred solution as it is mine – I have devised a companion lighting scheme that incorporates several innovative features.

As shown in the section looking north and in greater detail in the illustration accompanying this report, the essential element of this scheme is a 'light chamber' that runs around the perimeter of each gallery at the clerestory level. Daylight enters this chamber in a diffused form through a continuous translucent skylight and passes thence into the gallery below through translucent glazing in the clerestory. Because the light chamber is painted white, it is an extremely efficient reflector, assuring that approximately equal amounts of daylight enter the gallery from all sides, irrespective of the direction or angle of the sun. Sensor-controlled motor-operated opaque shades, mounted just beneath the skylight, provide sophisticated control over the amount of light that is allowed to enter the light chamber and permit total blackout during those daylight hours when the Gallery is not open to the public. The height and plan location of the clerestory are such as to direct the daylight onto the walls below at the optimum angle for viewing the pictures, with the largest amount of light falling in the hanging zone.

The light chamber also accommodates two types of supplemental artificial light: first, banks of fluorescent tubes, balanced in colour to match daylight, are installed in recesses along the walls of the chamber opposite the clerestory to provide supplemental general illumination when daylight is insufficient; and second, incandescent focal light fixtures, installed in a ceiling recess adjacent to and accessible from the chamber, provide special lighting supplemental to the general illumination if and as desired.

Aside from the fact that this light chamber provides optimum lighting for the paintings from both daylight and artificial sources, several other advantages may be cited:

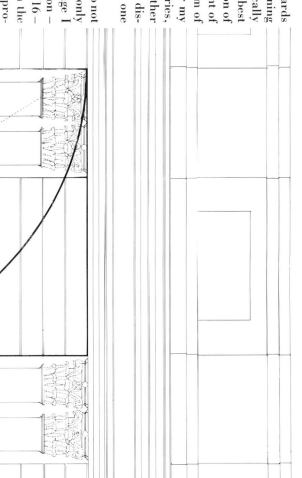
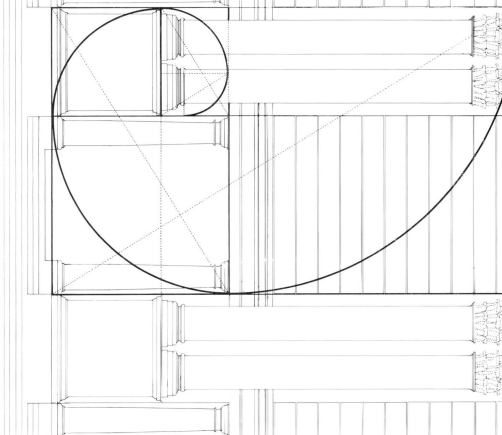

Proportional analysis of facade.

HENRY N COBB OF I M PEI & PARTNERS

# HENRY N COBB OF I M PEI & PARTNERS

1 The light chamber utilises a minimum area of exposed skylight to maximum effect.

2 Supplemental fluorescent light enters the gallery from concealed sources within the light chamber, thus appearing almost indistinguishable from daylight, rather than from exposed fixtures in the gallery ceiling.

3 The skylight is so located that there is no possibility of water leakage through it into the gallery below.

4 The light chamber is large enough for a man to walk upright inside it, and since all chambers are interconnected, the entire system and all elements installed in it are readily accessible for maintenance, repair or replacement without requiring internal scaffolding.

5 The light chamber is extremely adaptable, lending itself to installation of improved types of lighting that might become available in the future, without requiring extensive alteration or new construction.

*Gallery sequence:* The sequential arrangement of the exhibition galleries as shown in the gallery-level plan is as provisional as the 'ideal hang' on which it is based. Nonetheless, several aspects of this arrangement seem to me reasonably likely to prove valid irrespective of the specific programme to be applied. First, I believe that the designated point of arrival by stair is optimal in that it offers the visitor (whether coming from or going to the main building) immediate access to a number of internal destinations. There is no other location that can match it for convenience and clarity. Second, I believe that the logical place to begin the chronological exhibition sequence is in the northernmost gallery on axis at the head of the stairs, and that the sequence logically ends in the bridge gallery just east of the stair landing. Third, I believe that the square vestibule at the end of the long axis on the west side of the building is the logical place to offer visitors the choice between going 'south' to Group 4 or 'north' to Group 5. And finally, for reasons that must be obvious from my discussion of the exterior, I believe that the large altarpieces (Group 16) are best housed in a special room under the octagonal cupola at the southernmost end of the building.

Beyond these elements that seem logically fixed in place, I see the gallery-level plan as being open to a variety of different arrangements, particularly in the large central zone lying between the west vestibule where the choice is made between 'north' and 'south' and the octagonal cupola gallery containing the large altar-pieces. The arrangement which I have chosen to show in my plan is simply the product of my preliminary judgment about the balance to be struck between sequential clarity and opportunity for cross-referencing. I would not claim that this is the only or even necessarily the optimal arrangement, but I do believe it demonstrates that the pictures and groupings specified in the brief can indeed be accommodated and that the desired interconnections between 'north' and 'south' can indeed be made.

*The cupola gallery:* Aside from its obviously central role as the locus of large altarpieces, the cupola gallery is clearly the symbolic centre of the Hampton site extension – the singular place where its external volume and internal spatial configuration are powerfully joined to communicate a sense of its institutional purpose. It is of course no accident that the shape and material quality of this room, like the profile of its crowning cupola, evoke the mood of the Quattrocento. But whereas on the exterior that mood could only be hinted at behind a screen-wall which is principally concerned with addressing its urban context, here on the interior it is appropriate to make a much more explicit reference to that exhilarating moment in the art of architecture which accompanied an equally exhilarating moment in the art of painting. What to me is most compelling about the cupola gallery is the opportunity it affords to bring together the two opposite aspects of the building that I referred to earlier – its intimate engagement with the life of the city and its intimate engagement with the life of art – which thus can enlarge our understanding of both. And this explains why I have chosen to introduce into the ambulatory around the cupola gallery four narrow openings, set between the pilasters of the colossal order of the facade, which afford a glimpse – but only a glimpse – from the hushed interior with its Quattrocento ambiance into the twentieth-century hub-bub of the street below.

## Ancillary facilities

At this preliminary stage of design, my principal objective in allocating space to the ancillary facilities called for in the brief has been to achieve clarity and simplicity in the arrangement – qualities that are especially important in a programmatically complex building which is to be inhabited largely by first-time visitors. The entry sequence from the street to the permanent exhibition galleries, as has been described above, establishes an internal armature around which the ancillary facilities fall quite readily into place. Among these the temporary exhibitions gallery seems to me to merit both visual prominence and ease of access, and I have therefore located it at the northern end of the entrance lobby – a position in which it could easily be kept open to the public at times when the permanent exhibition galleries above are closed. This gallery takes the form of a large square room (24m by 24m by 5.5m high), with only four internal columns, thus accommodating a variety of exhibition layouts. Direct access is provided to this gallery from the service dock and goods lift.

The 400-seat lecture theatre is located immediately beneath the temporary exhibitions gallery (with columns relocated at this level to accommodate seating) and is reached by way of the main staircase that interconnects all levels of the building. Just outside the theatre is a generous lobby with a box office located on one side and a cloakroom and public toilets on the other. This lobby is only 2m below the grade-level entrance on Jubilee Walk, which thus becomes the logical point of access for evening events in the theatre.

The publications department shop is located at grade level, with display windows opening onto Jubilee Walk and with access provided from the Jubilee Walk entrance lobby. This shop also occupies basement space immediately below, with an internal connecting stair between the two levels. (The publications department goods-in area is located on the lower level between the shop and the goods lift.)

The restaurant is located just above the shop, overlooking Jubilee Walk and accessible from the main staircase landing between the entrance lobby and the permanent exhibitions galleries.

The audiovisual room is located beneath the circular entrance vestibule, whilst the information room is adjacent to the entrance lobby opposite the main staircase. And it should be noted that all of the ancillary facilities I have referred to are accessible not only by way of the main staircase but also by way of a nearby passenger elevator serving all levels within the building.

It will have been noticed that I have not provided in this design any of the 'optional' facilities mentioned in the guidelines – that is to say the boardroom suite, the publications department offices (though storage is provided), or the car park. I found that these facilities could not be accommodated without compromising some aspects of the building's public function to which I have elected to give a clear priority. Nonetheless, I believe the possibility of including at least the boardroom suite, perhaps on an upper floor just behind the Pall Mall frontage, could be further explored within the framework of the present scheme.

**The National Gallery in Trafalgar Square** I want to conclude this report by returning once more to the exterior and considering how the Hampton site extension, as I have envisioned it, may act together

with the main building to create a new presence for the National Gallery in Trafalgar Square. As indicated in the scale model, I have followed through on the proposal that I made last September to eliminate the raised lawn across the entire front of the main building, thus allowing the stairs from the main portico to descend laterally as well as frontally to the footpath. In the greatly expanded pavement area thus created, a mutually complementary dialogue takes place between the two porticos – a dialogue in which the present main portico continues to assert its primacy overlooking the Square, while the portico of the new extension exerts an appropriately powerful attraction for the pedestrian at street level. It seems to me that both the external posture and the internal chronological arrangement of the newly expanded museum complex will tend to encourage visitors to enter at street level through the Hampton site extension and to exit onto the raised portico of the main building, with its splendid vista into Trafalgar Square and down Whitehall to Westminster.

But whatever the route chosen by visitors to the exhibition galleries, they and casual passers-by alike will benefit from the enlarged and enriched open space offered by the National Gallery to London's public realm. In shaping its new presence in that public realm the Gallery's main building and the extension to the west play complementary and interdependent roles. Indeed, as I remarked in my initial site analysis, one of the perceived weaknesses of the main building – its compositional looseness and ambivalence – becomes a positive asset in the context of the Hampton site extension. To understand why this is so, it is necessary only to consider how much more difficult it would have been to design a satisfactory extension on this site had Wilkins been allowed to execute his preferred design, with its imposing colonnaded porticos, in place of the cupola capped pavilions that now punctuate the flanking wings. My discovery of the opportunity for engendering a lateral movement outwards from this otherwise overwhelmingly frontal facade was the beginning of my understanding of the architectural possibilities of the Hampton site extension. Last September, when I first discussed this discovery with the committee, I had only the most general idea where it might lead. The work accomplished in the intervening months, aside from giving me a great deal of pleasure, has given me a confidence born of conviction that the committee's wish for an extension to the National Gallery that would be 'distinct from the existing building but belong to it' can become a wish fulfilled.

*Henry Nichols Cobb*

Perspective view from Trafalgar Square.

HENRY N COBB OF I M PEI & PARTNERS

# Colquhoun + Miller with RMJM

These proposals are presented purely as a reconnaissance. We have included all the accommodation asked for in the guidelines, even though in some instances the required areas have not quite been achieved. We felt that it was only by developing one scheme to a fair degree of detail that the brief could be tested against the available area. Whether or not we are successful, we believe that such an investigation will be helpful in the further development of the brief.

**The historical context**

During the past decade there has been a major change of attitude on the part of the commissioning public and the architectural profession as to the proper relationship between a new building and its context.

Following the wholesale destruction of inner cities in the name of modernity, it is now generally accepted that the external form of new buildings should respect the historical structure of the city, rather than seek to adumbrate some utopian city of the second machine age.

In many ways the National Gallery extension has come to be seen as a test case of this new attitude, and as such it poses the important question of the language and character appropriate to a new public building on a prestigious site, and in close proximity to an existing building of historical and aesthetic significance.

In approaching this problem we have been guided by a number of general principles.

— A modern building should not be a clone of an old building (any more than a

modern novel should exactly imitate the style of Balzac or Dickens).

— Any city is made up of buildings of different periods, each of which was once a 'modern' addition to the urban context.

— The word 'context' should be taken to mean not only the actual physical context (in this case Wilkins' National Gallery, Smirke's Canada House, Trafalgar Square, St Martin's, etc), but also those general architectural ideas which constitute the raw material out of which a new building is made — the 'architectural tradition'.

— We have seen the context — taken in this broad sense — as consisting of a set of underlying, but freely interpreted, grammatical elements. Among these are: the wall and its articulation, string courses, cornices, windows, columns, lintels,

arches. In adapting these elements to the National Gallery extension we have not hesitated to make use of historical precedents.

**The urban context**

The site for the National Gallery extension is of unique importance. The new building will have to take its place among a collection of well-known monumental buildings which are disposed around Trafalgar Square like a series of chess pieces. The building should itself have a monumental character, but should respect the scale and character of its neighbours, especially Wilkins' National Gallery and Smirke's Canada House.

The design submitted has attempted to reconcile the need for a monumental building with the need for a building that

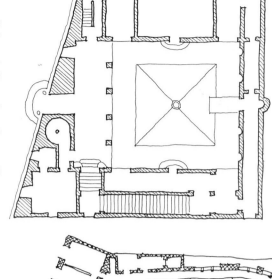

Palazzo in Rome from Letarouilly.

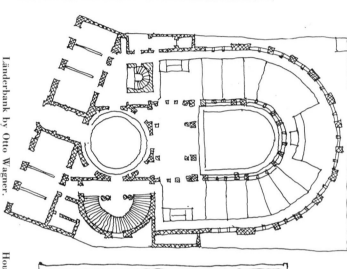

Länderbank by Otto Wagner.

Houses in Rome from Letarouilly showing straight flight staircase and exedra as used in the ground-floor and mezzanine lobbies of the National Gallery extension.

is 'context sensitive'.

Our main concern has been to give the building a simple form, and not to fragment it in response to supposed contextual pressures. In this way the building will respond to the more general context of the palace type of building prevalent in this part of London.

One of the reasons for this block-like treatment of the building is the need to continue the alignment of Pall Mall East and to form a visual stop to the northwest corner of Trafalgar Square. A further reason is the need to maximise the use of the site.

In considering the relation of the new building to the old National Gallery, Canada House, and the general character of Pall Mall East, various solutions were tried out.

As a result of these studies the following decisions were made.

— The east frontage of the new building should be rotated so that its two long sides are parallel, thus reducing the accidental character of the site.

— The bridge between the new and the old building should have a strong architectural form so as to mediate between the two buildings.

— The footpath should be a positive space. 'To this end the new building has been made to respond symmetrically to the west pavilion of the old building to form a 'gateway'.

— The main entrance should be on Pall Mall East.

— The new building should continue the line of the entablature and plinth of the old building, though in a simplified form. Between these lines the facade of the new building should be different from the old and express its own internal organisation.

— Top-lit galleries would result in a top floor largely without windows.

— The new building should respond to the National Gallery by dividing the main facade into a centre portion and two side pavilions. We found that one of the main problems was to avoid a unit of scale too large for the staccato rhythm of the Wil-

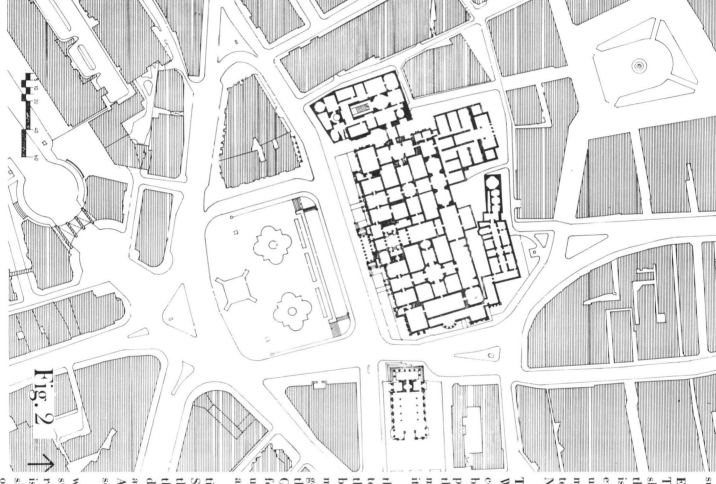

Site plan.

Fig.2

kins facade, which has always been the subject of some criticism.

**External finishes**

The external finishes of the new building should be sympathetic to the materials of the surrounding buildings. To this end it is proposed to finish the plinth of the extension in unpolished granite and the upper portions in Portland stone. These materials respond to those used in the terrace wall of Trafalgar Square and the National Gallery respectively.

**The wider urban context**

We have not considered the problems connected with the wider urban context to the National Gallery. One solution to this would be to pedestrianise the road bounding the north of the Square. A more modest solution, and one which we suggest in our proposals, would be to widen the pavement in front of the National Gallery. This would also provide space for a stairway leading to a pedestrian underpass between the existing building and the Square.

A greater problem is the lack of definition to the south edge of Trafalgar Square. This results, historically, from the fact that Nash's layout of 1824 used the existing mediaeval street pattern to define the south side. The subsequent addition of openings to Northumberland Avenue and Admiralty Arch eroded the south edge even further.

Any radical solution to the problem would entail the deployment of very substantial political powers and financial resources. At present, the least one can do is to preserve the geometry of the north side of the Square. This we have done in our proposals for the siting of the extension.

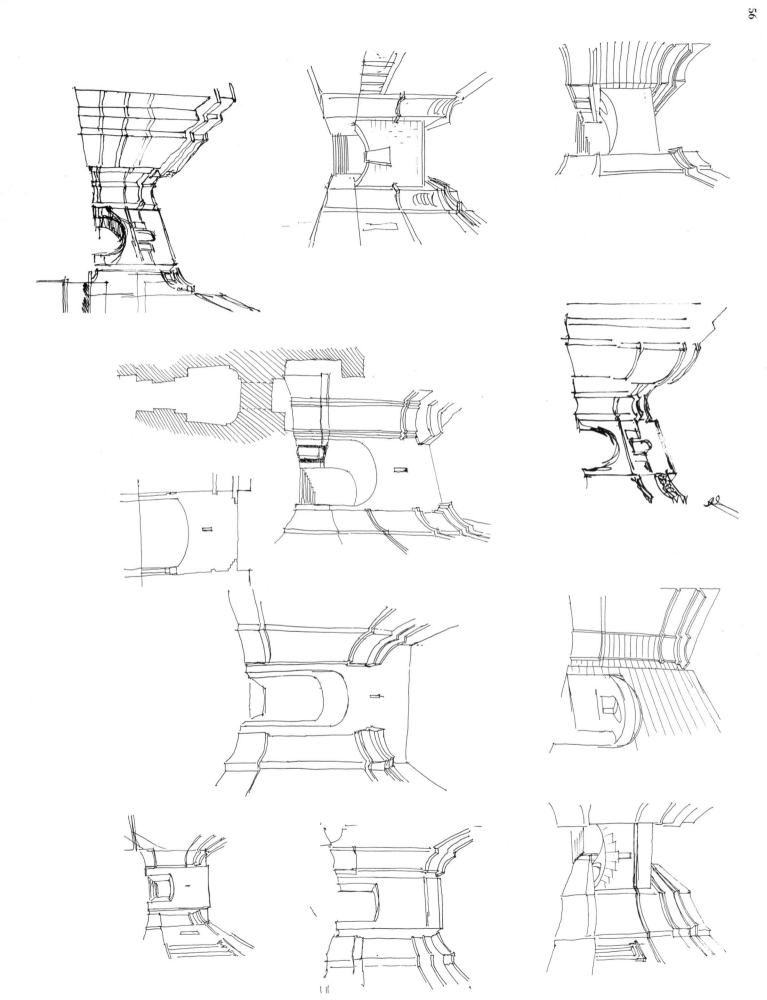

right of way

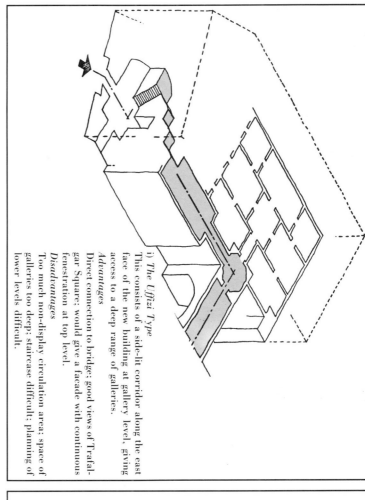

### i) *The Uffizi Type*

This consists of a side-lit corridor along the east face of the new building at gallery level, giving access to a deep range of galleries.

*Advantages*

Direct connection to bridge; good views of Trafalgar Square; would give a facade with continuous fenestration at top level.

*Disadvantages*

Too much non-display circulation area; space of galleries too deep; staircase difficult; planning of lower levels difficult.

---

### ii) *The Side Cascade Type*

Developed to overcome difficulties of staircase position in the Uffizi type. It has the same advantages and one additional disadvantage — that of cutting out natural light from the mezzanine on the east face.

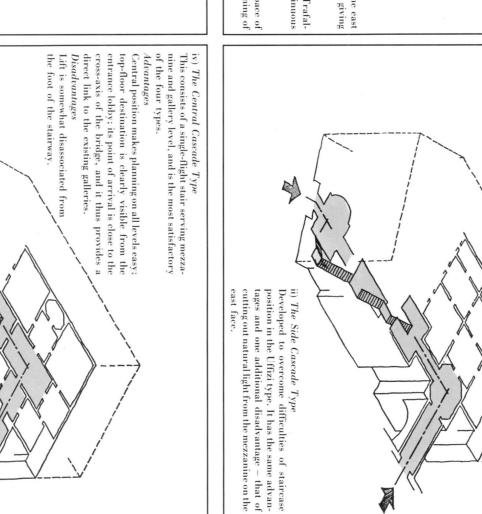

---

### iii) *The Rotunda Type*

*Advantages*

Central position makes planning on all levels easy; provides a dramatic 'core' that would help orientate the visitor; maximises gallery area; provides natural light to ground floor.

*Disadvantages*

Constriction at point of entry to rotunda; point of arrival of stair at gallery level too far from bridge.

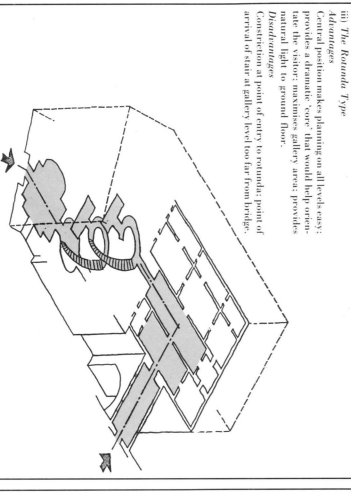

---

### iv) *The Central Cascade Type*

This consists of a single-flight stair serving mezzanine and gallery level, and is the most satisfactory of the four types.

*Advantages*

Central position makes planning on all levels easy; top-floor destination is clearly visible from the entrance lobby; its point of arrival is close to the cross-axis of the bridge, and it thus provides a direct link to the existing galleries.

*Disadvantages*

Lift is somewhat disassociated from the foot of the stairway.

## The planning of the interior: alternative schemes

The chief aim of the plan organisation has been to make the main public spaces easily and clearly accessible to each other and from the entrance lobby.

A number of variant plans were considered and four of these were examined in greater detail. They differ from each other in their main circulation systems, and can best be described as: *The Uffizi*, *The Side Cascade*, *The Rotunda*, and *The Central Cascade*.

## Description of the chosen scheme (central cascade): schematic plan

The plan consists of a top floor of galleries below which all the other accommodation is stacked.

A straight flight of stairs on the north-south axis leads from the entrance lobby to the gallery level.

The temporary exhibition space and the lecture theatre occupy the centre of the ground floor and the basement. The remainder of the accommodation is wrapped around the temporary exhibition space, taking advantage of peripheral natural light.

Within this broad schema, various alternative arrangements of the accommodation are possible. Our proposal shows one such arrangement.

### The lecture theatre

This is located in the basement and is accessible by means of a generous open stair at the west end of the vestibule, and also by means of the lifts.

### The temporary exhibition

This occupies the centre of the plan at ground-floor level. It is directly accessible from the vestibule. We have shown a separate entrance from the public footpath because we feel that the large numbers of visitors to temporary exhibitions should probably be kept separate from visitors to permanent collections. Security problems connected with multiple entries might, however, argue against this provision.

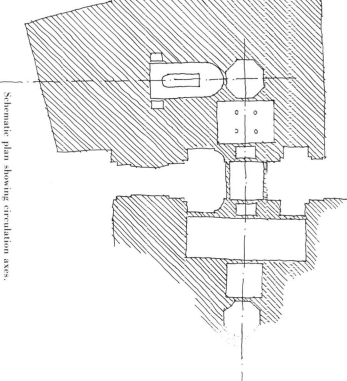

Schematic plan showing circulation axes.

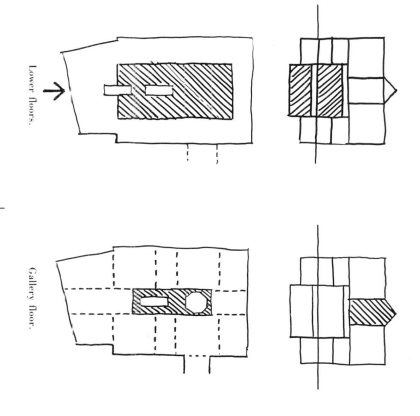

Lower floors.

Gallery floor.

### Audiovisual room

This is located on the ground floor between the temporary exhibition space and the entrance lobby. It is directly accessible from both.

### The bookshop

This has been located on the Whitcomb Street frontage to take advantage of the pedestrian traffic on the street. It was felt that this outweighed the possible disadvantage in placing the shop at the furthest point from the existing Gallery. It is assumed that most people visiting the shop from the existing Gallery will in any case approach it from the bridge.

### The restaurant

This is on the mezzanine level and occupies the entire Pall Mall East frontage. It is accessible from a lobby at the half-landing of the main stair, and is thus mid-way between the vestibule and the gallery floor. It has views across Pall Mall east, and diagonally to Trafalgar Square.

### The Trustees' suite

This is at mezzanine level on the east frontage of the building. It is accessible from the half landing of the main stair, as well as from a private entrance, on the public footpath. The boardroom, being adjacent to the service lift, is conveniently placed for delivery of paintings for viewing. It has a large north window facing onto St Martin's Street, providing good lighting for viewing paintings.

In addition to the above the following accommodation is provided: *basement* – parking for seven cars, plant room, warden's accommodation, public toilets, storage; *ground floor* – service entrance and loading bay, cloakroom, security office; *mezzanine* – publications office, kitchen, public toilets.

## The planning of the galleries

The gallery floor is traversed by two axes of circulation, one from the stair and one from the bridge. Visitors can pass directly from the entrance lobby of the new building to the gallery floor of the old building, or vice-versa.

The axes from the stair and from the bridge converge on an octagonal space which is the starting point of the exhibition sequence. The visitor can start at the beginning of the exhibition sequence whether approaching from the stair or the bridge.

Our proposal shows one possible arrangement of galleries, namely chronologically beginning with Groups 1, 2 and 3, and then splitting into two streams: the Italian and the Northern. It is possible to make a cross-reference between the earlier Italian Schools and Netherlandish Realism. The hinge of this cross-connection is the gallery containing the paintings of Piero della Francesco and Joos.

## Information room

This room is located at the south end of the gallery floor. It is treated as a studio space, and has a mezzanine. It receives natural light from windows at the upper level.

## The rooms and their character

The galleries consist of interconnecting galleries which vary in size and shape partly as a result of their position in the plan and partly as a result of the requirements of the 'ideal hang'.

The studies show a variety of plan arrangements that have been investigated. They also show an undivided plan indicating the structural and immoveable walls. It is assumed that frequent changes of wall position would be unlikely. Changes in the long term may be necessary, and care has been taken to position structural and mechanical elements so that such changes would not be impeded.

## Special paintings

A possible arrangement of 'outstanding' paintings is shown. These are placed within bays or niches, on important axes, or in separate rooms.

Most of the galleries are 5.5m high to underside of cove but some of the smaller galleries have lower ceilings.

There is a lobby in the southeast corner of the building which has a view of the old National Gallery and Trafalgar Square. This lobby would provide a resting place about halfway round the circuit. Slightly more than 500m run of hanging wall is provided by this layout.

## COLQUHOUN + MILLER WITH RMJM

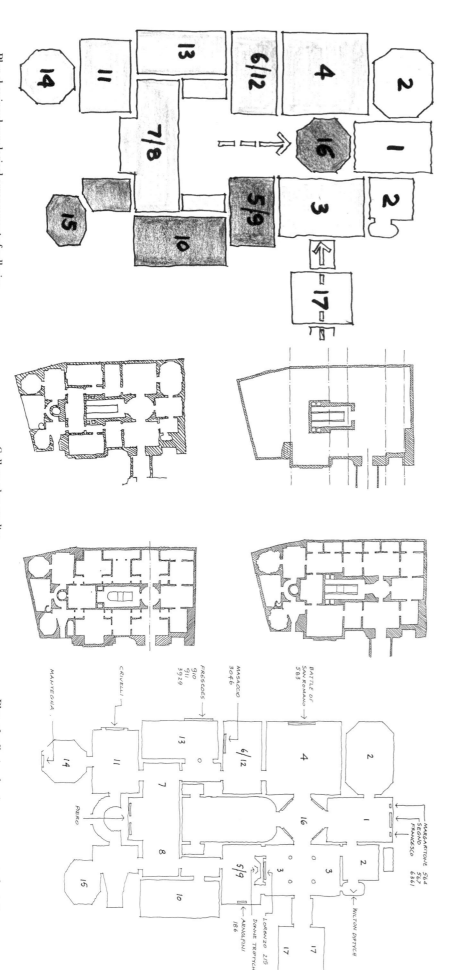

Plan showing chronological arrangement of galleries.

Gallery plan studies.

Plan of galleries showing arrangement of paintings.

## Finishes and decoration

It is intended that there should be a uniform system of floor and wall finishes and architraves throughout the galleries. Within this dominant system, however, there would be room for variations of floor pattern, wall colouring and so on, to reinforce the character of particular groups of paintings.

We would propose a 1m wide margin round all rooms, probably in a light-coloured marble, so as to reflect light up onto the lower parts of the walls. The centre of each room would probably be in strip or block wood of a medium tone, though carpet might be considered. The line of the margin would also be the line of any guard rail required to protect the paintings.

The walls would be plastered to give a rough texture similar to that found in many Italian galleries.

The exact colour of the walls would have to be the subject of careful study by the client and the architect, though a near-white suggests itself for the majority of galleries.

To give a special character to certain rooms (eg Netherlandish Realism) such variations as checked stone floor, or coloured walls, might be considered. Generally speaking, however, we would be against stylistic changes to 'sympathise' with particular paintings. The overriding objective of the decorative scheme would be to create a good background for paintings.

The entrance lobby staircase and upper-level stair lobby would have walls and floors finished in stone.

## Daylighting to galleries

In these proposals our aim has been to avoid a bland and monotonous effect and to design a system that, while keeping broadly within the prescribed range of lux values, would make the viewer aware of the changing conditions of the sky.

Our proposals assume daylight as the principal source of illumination supplemented with artificial light where necessary. Owing to the varying shape and orientation of the different galleries, there would be subtly different light conditions in each, thus helping to avoid a 'gallery fatigue'.

In recent years much research has been done on the physical effect of light on paintings, resulting in the establishment of quantitative standards, the need for UV filtration and so on.

The question of the psychological effect of lighting on the viewer, however, is of equal importance and has more bearing on the architectural qualities of the building, and the well-being of the viewer.

Our researches so far have indicated that the best way to achieve a lively and efficient system of daylighting is to channel the light onto the wall surface, and to

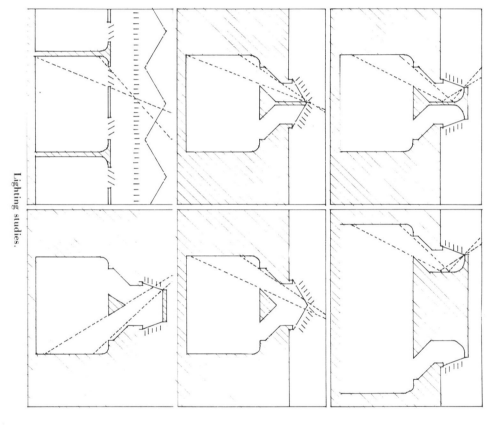

Lighting studies.

reduce the amount of light falling on the centre of the floor. This can be achieved via slots around the perimeter of the ceiling, set off by about 1m from the wall surface.

The depth of about 2m required by the roof structure gives sufficient depth for the light entering the room to be reflected off the vertical surfaces of the slot above ceiling level.

We have shown lanterns over all roof lights because these enable the louvres to be fixed to vertical glazing, thus reducing the amount of direct sunlight to be countered and allowing the louvres always to remain partly open.

In this system there is a danger of the appearance of a heavy light-control mechanism hovering over the middle of the room. This, however, can be avoided by firmly establishing the ceiling plane, and penetrating it with discontinuous slots.

Such a system is proposed for all galleries except those of octagonal shape. In these there would be central lanterns, with prismatic laylights to direct the light onto the walls.

## Artificial light

Although it is no doubt too early to decide on the kind of light fittings to be used, our experience at the Whitechapel Art Gallery suggests that it is possible to achieve an even distribution of light on a wall surface by means of a single fluorescent tube mounted in a parabolic reflector, recessed in the ceiling. This would be one of the possibilities to be investigated.

Most probably such a system would be supplemented with incandescent spot lights fixed to flush tracks. These spots would be mounted so as to be outside the normal range of vision of the viewer, thus avoiding the confusing effect of spot lights at various angles so frequent in galleries.

## Problems of adaptability

In considering alterations in the long term there might be an advantage in separating the function of light admission (and therefore the design of the ceiling configuration) from the function of weather-proofing. This could be achieved by means of a continuous 'greenhouse' roof over all the galleries, but careful study of the cost implications of such a solution and the effect on heat loss and gain would have to be made.

Because of the probable infrequency of change we do not favour a modular ceiling pattern that could remain constant throughout all changes of wall position. Rather, top lighting has been tailored to the individual rooms, and it is accepted that changes in room sizes would necessitate corresponding alterations in ceiling configuration.

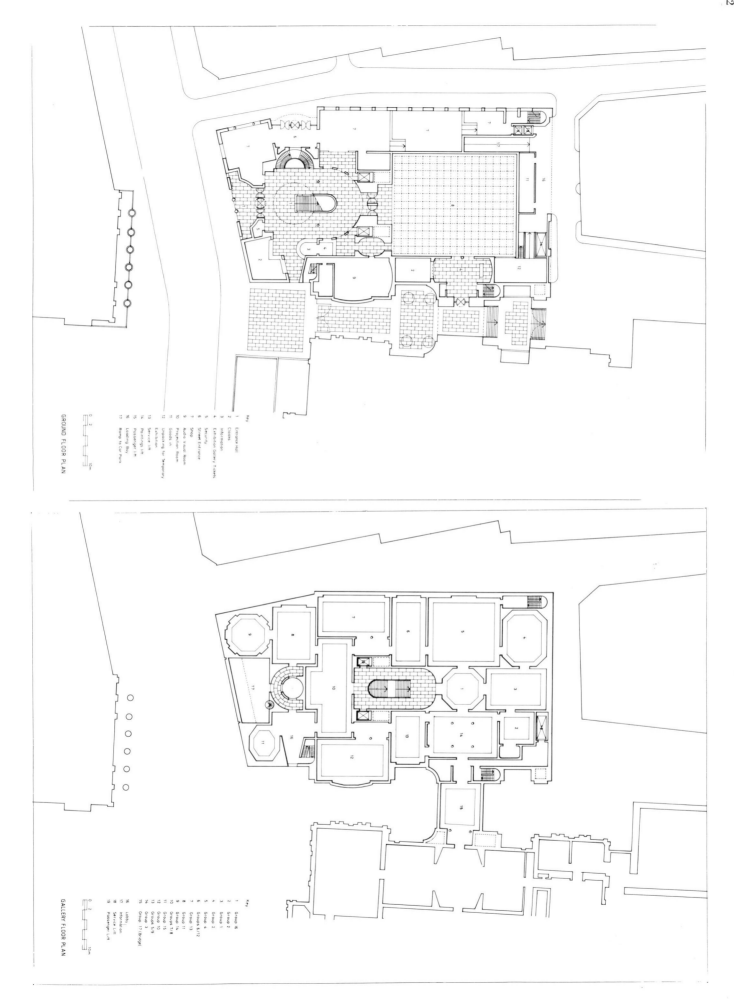

GROUND FLOOR PLAN

0 2 10m

Key

1 Entrance Hall
2 Cloaks
3 Information
4 Exhibition Gallery Tickets
5 Security
6 Street Entrance
7 Shop
8 Audio Visual Room
9 Projection Room
10 Goods In
11 Unpacking for Temporary
12 Exhibition
13 Service Lift
14 Paintings Lift
15 Passenger Lift
16 Loading Bay
17 Ramp to Car Park

GALLERY FLOOR PLAN

0 2 10m

Key

1 Group 16
2 Group 2
3 Group 1
4 Group 2
5 Group 4
6 Groups 6/12
7 Group 13
8 Group 11
9 Groups 14
10 Groups 7/8
11 Group 15
12 Group 10
13 Group 3
14 Groups 5/9
15 Group 17 (Bridge)
16 Lobby
17 Information
18 Service Lift
19 Passenger Lift

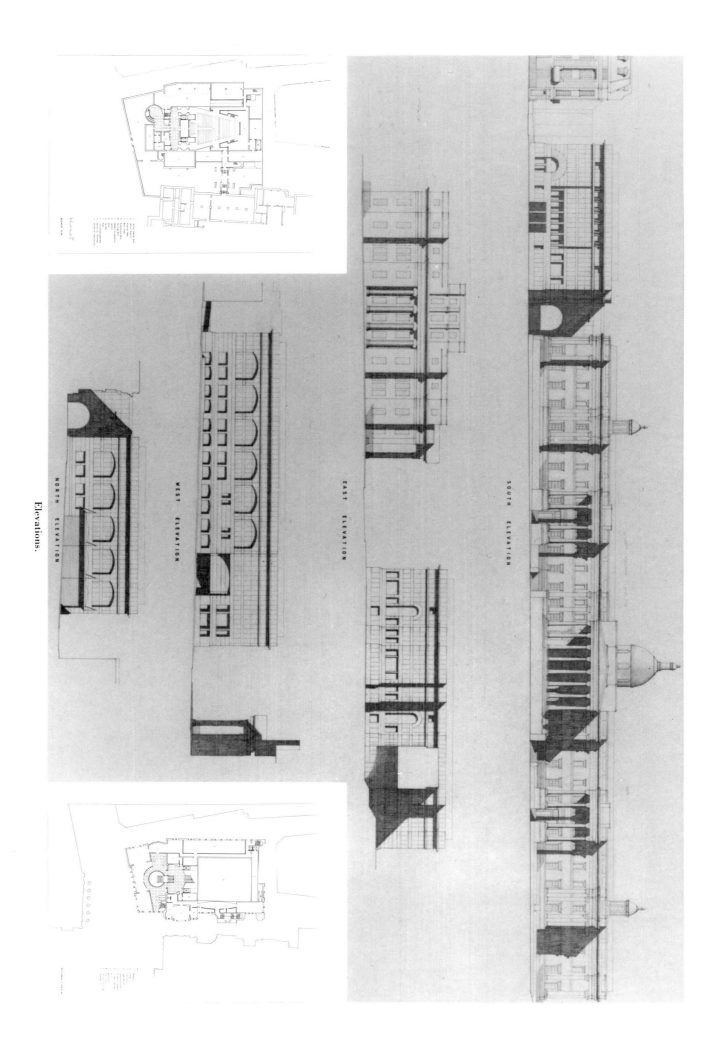

Elevations.

COLQUHOUN + MILLER WITH RMJM

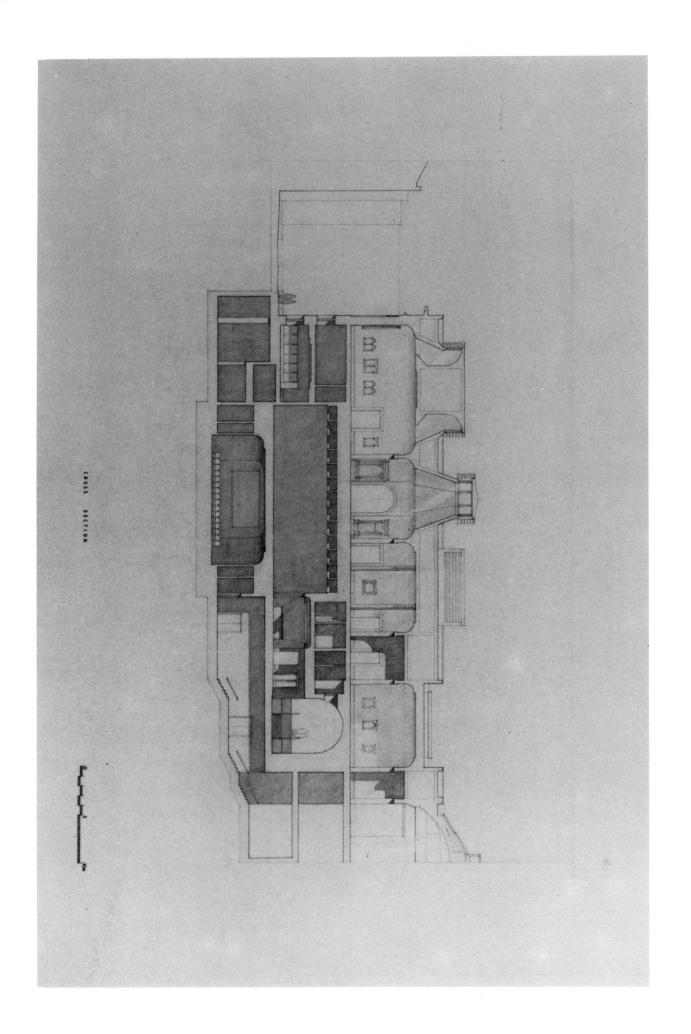

CROSS SECTION

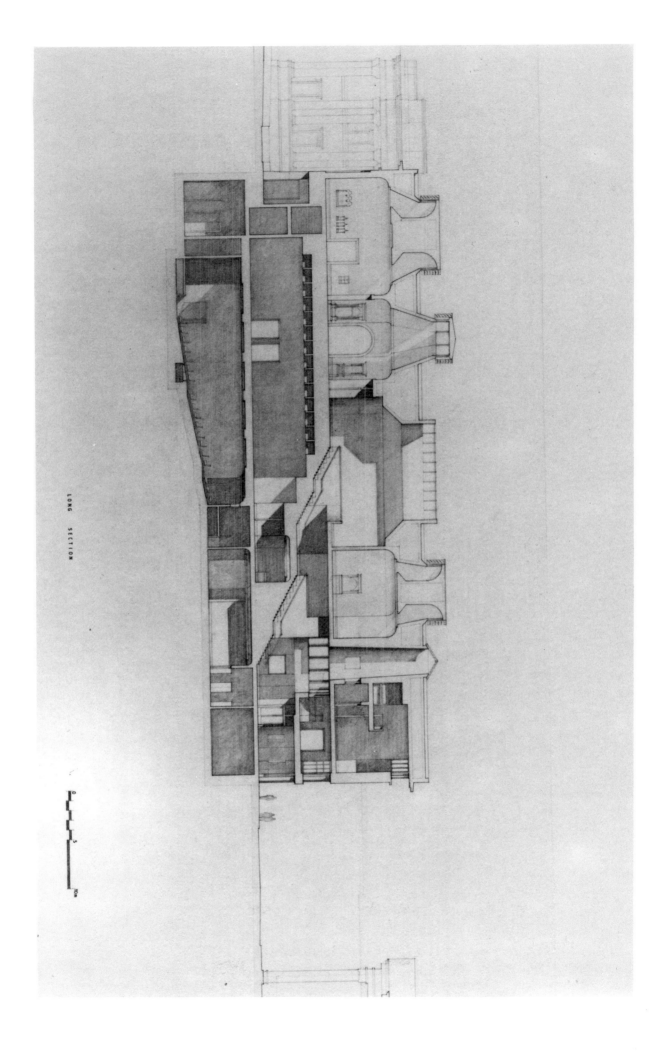

LONG SECTION

COLQUHOUN + MILLER WITH RMJM

Perspective section through entrance hall.

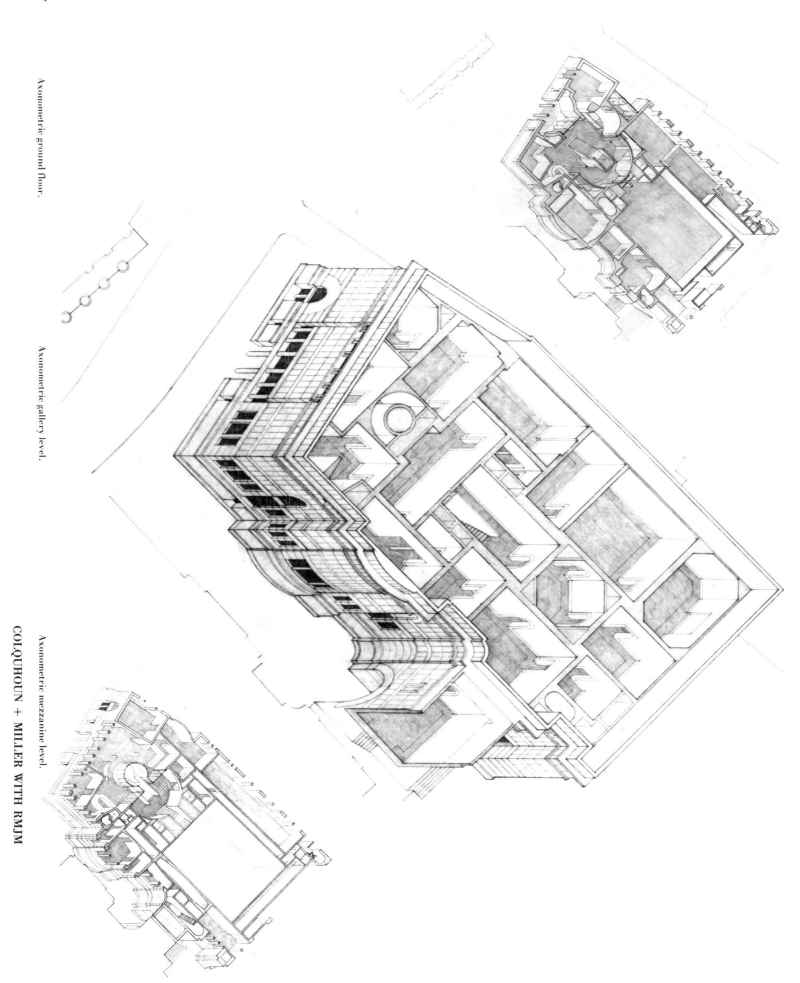

Axonometric ground floor.

Axonometric gallery level.

Axonometric mezzanine level.

**COLQUHOUN + MILLER WITH RMJM**

VIEW FROM NORTH WEST CORNER OF SQUARE

COLQUHOUN + MILLER WITH RMJM

VIEW FROM NORTH EAST CORNER .OF SQUARE

COLQUHOUN + MILLER WITH RMJM

# James Stirling,
# Michael Wilford & Associates

NATIONAL GALLERY EXTENSION
HAMPTON SITE. LONDON

Our proposal for the National Gallery Extension is presented as a theme with variations.   We hope this approach
indicates an ability to respond to differing criteria without loss of architectural control, - possibly an
important requirement in coping with a yet to be finalised brief.   This is our primary reason for adopting
this procedure.

The more generous and spacious Scheme A is our preference and our proposal.   It accommodates the maximum brief
including the Publications Department and a Boardroom Suite and has some additional admin. spaces.   We think
it responds to the likelihood of ever larger public and ancillary spaces being required in a popular Museum.

The variations adapt to the same building footprint and have approx. the same building volume above ground and
they use the same system of roof lighting through scoops.   A and B have similar gallery plans with commencement
of the gallery sequence starting above the entrance of the new building, whereas C proposes a circulation through
the new galleries commencing at the link with the existing National Gallery.   Variation B has the Temporary
Exhibition space at the same level as the Entrance Hall.   In A it is below, where it can be larger in size.

To an extent there may be interchangeable elements - for instance the shop/street entrance arrangement as shown
on A could be applied in B.   Similarly the Pall Mall bay windows and the entrance canopies could be interchanged.

This project has been developed assuming the most onerous planning constraints.   If the frontage on Whitcomb Street
could be adjusted to achieve a 50/50 give and take over the parapet line, there would be a corresponding increase
in gallery area.

JAMES STIRLING MICHAEL WILFORD and ASSOCIATES

---

ADDENDUM - INTERVIEW NOTES
STIRLING WILFORD & ASSOCIATES
Scheme A

Our report is factual and I hope self explanatory, nevertheless an introduction might have been an asset and I
would like to attempt this now as a preface to clarifying details of our submission.

There are many ways of 'reading' the front of the National Gallery, which personally I like, as primarily I think
of it's facade as being a long wall containing the top side of Trafalgar Square.   There is however at the right
end of this wall a definite stop caused by the front of St Martin in the Fields and this front faces sideways
towards the Gallery and obliquely towards the square.   To an extent in a similar way we hope to terminate the
left end of the National Gallery wall and complete the overall balancing act with the presence of our building.
Like St Martin's we hope our building is an architectural entity and, though influenced by the design of the
National Gallery, only in a limited way does it pick up elements from the existing building;  - most particularly
the plinth and the cornice.

The wall of the National Gallery is animated by columns, pilasters - and the back-and-forth movement of pavilions
so that, when viewed at any particular place it has, locally, a vertical emphasis.   This is particularly the
case with the corner adjoining the Hampton site.   Conversely we are trying to give our facade a horizontal
emphasis in order to establish a somewhat different personality to that of the adjoining building.   Our Portland
stone facade is articulated by five recessed horizontal courses, - recessed about 2"; which combined with the
projecting plinth and cornice produces a horizontal emphasis.   This conjunction of the horizontality of the
new building with the vertical corner of the National Gallery can be seen by viewing the model, as it were from
the square.   The elevation drawings in the report are a first pass at proportions - and I feel the cornice may
be too prominent and the bay windows on Pall Mall too large.   However, our intention is to have a bottom, the
plinth, and a middle with horizontal  courses and a top with cornice.   Viewed from the steps of the National
Gallery the new building may have a more special reading - the emphasis of the gable end incorporating the void
of the entrance gives the building a face, - a face looking sideways towards the National Gallery and beyond to
St Martin in the Fields, and obliquely into the square.   The projecting canopy on the model is not right - it
should be more symmetric or less symmetric - or perhaps not exist if the building's soffit above the entrance
steps was considered able to provide enough cover.

The circular form of the entrance steps is able to receive pedestrians coming from all directions - westwards
from Pall Mall;  eastwards from the direction of the National Gallery and northwards from the footpath.   We
think of the area in front of these steps as a small plaza.   The half way landing of the steps is a place, perhaps
a stage, where visitors can converse - or perform, or just sit about - as happens on the steps of the Metropolitan
in New York and to some extent at the Tate.

I would like to think of our building on Pall Mall as a small palazzo, though also as the head on a body where the rest of the anatomy does not have the same density of external features.   There is a reducing hierarchy of architectural elements diminishing in intensity backwards from the most meaningful facade facing the square to the functional treatment of the elevation at the back, though here, the Publications entrance as viewed down St Martin's Street could be more elaborated.   It might also be architecturally more interesting not to carry the stone veneering of the building around every surface and northwards from the first or second step outs in the plan;  the elevations could be finished in stucco (or brick) which would be a considerable cost saving.

Neither the model or axonometric drawings show roof lanterns above galleries and the roof plane is shown as a neutral surface as the barely visible roofs. as seen from the ground, will not contribute to the architectural composition.   This is similar to the roof treatment of the National Gallery;  it seems the English Museum tradition is to conceal roofs behind parapets as distinct from the French way.   However the roof lanterns are shown on elevation and section drawings.

When Portland stone is used as a modern surface material it can be very bland, - partly due to the absence of decoration.   Large flat surfaces of other stones such as travertine, and sandstone, as we used them in Stuttgart can be very lively.   This is another reason for making recessed horizontal courses.   The courses might be of some other type of stone - maybe Bath stone.

The Galleries are intended as a set of regular, calm, dignified rooms - with any architectural expression being mainly confined to the design of the openings between rooms.   These openings do not have rooflit scoops over as there are no paintings here and, it is in these positions that the crossing of the services and access into the lanterns occur.   The controls, switches, telephones etc. required for each gallery would be accommodated in concealed cupboards within the side jambs of these openings.

The bridge link gallery is somewhat different in character, it has two openings either side of a vista stop wall and this causes a small detour or hiccup in the flow of visitors coming from the existing building and vice versa.   Adjoining this room are bay windows with seats and these will contribute to the feeling of difference at this special place in the combined gallery sequence.

The location of higher and lower galleries - as also the method of daylight/artificial lighting of galleries and the selection of finishes and colours etc. would be developed and decided in conjunction with the gallery experts.

In addition to the lifts a monumental three flight staircase connects all levels.   This stair has narrower flights on the flanks and a wider flight in the centre and the direction of the flights in effect points the flow of visitors backwards or forwards towards the primary spaces;  or equally in both directions where the Lecture Theatre and Temporary Exhibition rooms are at the same level.

The Banner hanging tripod is not essential to the architectural composition, though it does conveniently fit behind the splayed out pavement boundary on Pall Mall.   Banners could face both directions and sightlines would allow them to be seen from more than half the surface of Trafalgar Square.   They could have three messages - at the top referring to the presence of the National Gallery and at the bottom to the proximity of the Bookshop.   The largest area in the middle could change in colour and information according to current exhibitions.   It would be entirely up to the Gallery to consider whether they think this is a feature worth having.

It has been unusual producing a scheme without normal contact with the Client.   In reference to all aspects of the design achieved so far and in regard to the future development of the project we would hope for a Building Committee to be fully involved to aid, propose, support and approve every aspect of the design and development.

Note

The photos of the model on p.2. and 3 of the report are somewhat crude.   Though one doesn't focus on crudities of function and alignment when looking at the building in the context of the whole model;  however in these photos which focus on part of the model the inaccuracies are highlighted.   Possibly they should not have been included as the perspective on p.3. shows more accurately how we intend the architecture to look.

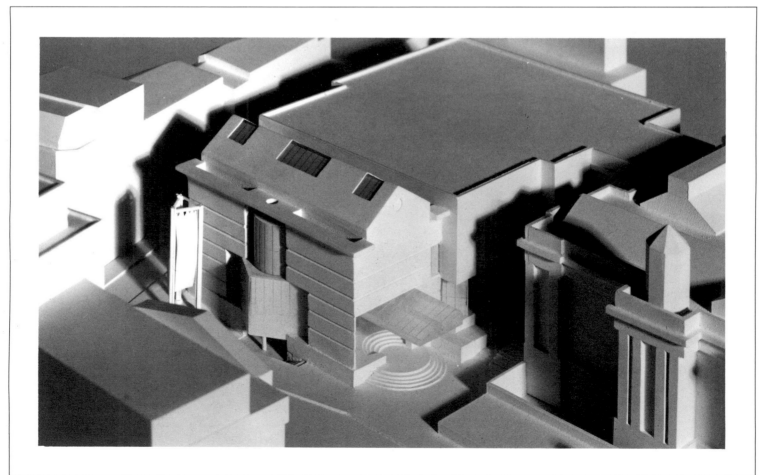

SCHEME A
ACCOMMODATION

| | | NATIONAL GALLERY GUIDELINES (m²) | AREAS ACHIEVED (m²) |
|---|---|---|---|
| 3.1 | GALLERIES | 1320 plus<br>wall length - 400m plus | 1640 (24% increase)* net<br>585m (46% increase)* |
| 3.2 | ENTRANCE VESTIBULE AND CLOAKROOM | 'spacious' | 710 |
| 3.3 | LECTURE THEATRE | 400 seats | 400 seats |
| 3.4 | PUBLICATIONS SHOP + STORE | 400 | 465 |
| 3.5 | RESTAURANT | min 150 seats | 185 seats |
| 3.6 | TEMPORARY EXHIBITION GALLERY + STORE | 700 - 1000 | 1010 net |
| 3.7 | AUDIO VISUAL | 100 - 150 seats | 125 seats |
| 3.8 | INFORMATION ROOM | 150 | 120 |
| 3.9 | MISC.<br>Warders Accommodation<br>Public Toilets<br>Service Entrance | 100<br>-<br>- | 100<br>195<br>420 ( 3 trucks ) |

or if a 1 gallery/bridge link = 1500 (14% increase)* net
525m (31% increase)*

--------------------------------------------------------------------

| | | | |
|---|---|---|---|
| 3.10 | BOARDROOM, DINING AND COMMITTEE ROOM | 200 | 220 |
| 3.11 | PUBLICATIONS DEPARTMENT<br>Offices<br>Storage | 400<br>200 | 560<br>200 |
| 3.12 | CAR PARKING | approx. 12 | 10 on St Martin's St. |

ACCOMMODATION ALSO PROVIDED:

a)  Cloakroom and Tickets for
    Temporary Exhibitions                        -                          50

b)  Administration and Service Offices           -                         165

A1

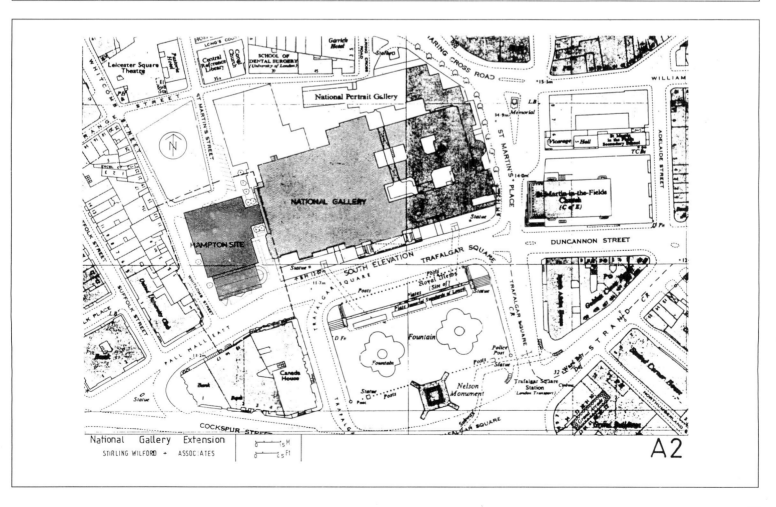

National Gallery Extension

STIRLING WILFORD + ASSOCIATES

A2

A3

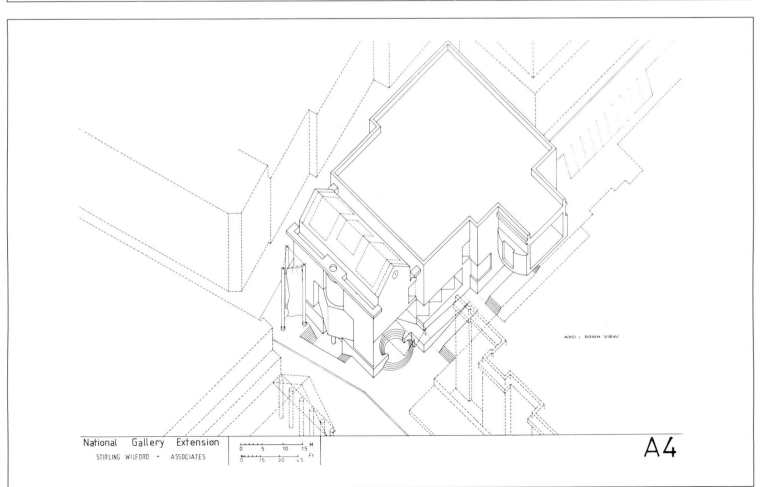

AXO : DOWN VIEW

National Gallery Extension
STIRLING WILFORD + ASSOCIATES

A4

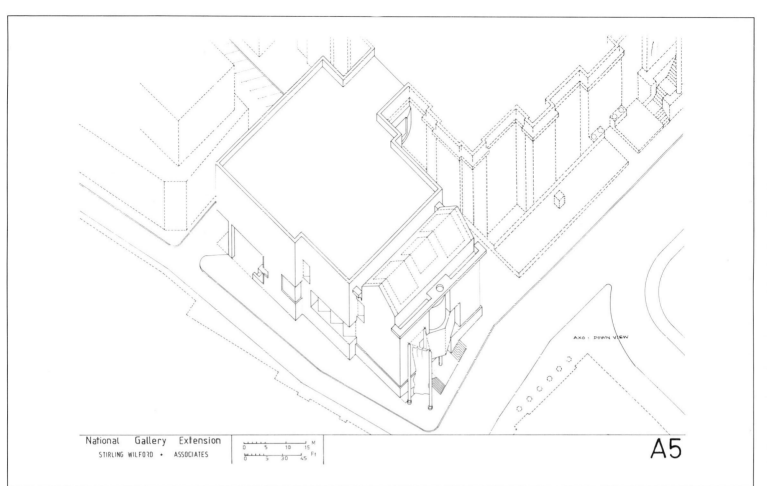

AXO : DOWN VIEW

National Gallery Extension
STIRLING WILFORD + ASSOCIATES

| 0 | 5 | 10 | 15 | M |
| 0 | 5 | 30 | 45 | Ft |

A5

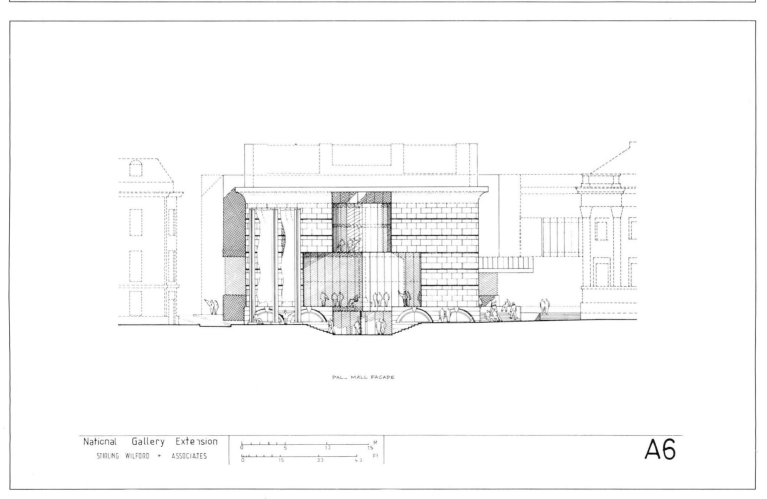

PALL MALL FACADE

National Gallery Extension
STIRLING WILFORD + ASSOCIATES

| 0 | 5 | 10 | 15 | M |
| 0 | 15 | 30 | 45 | Ft |

A6

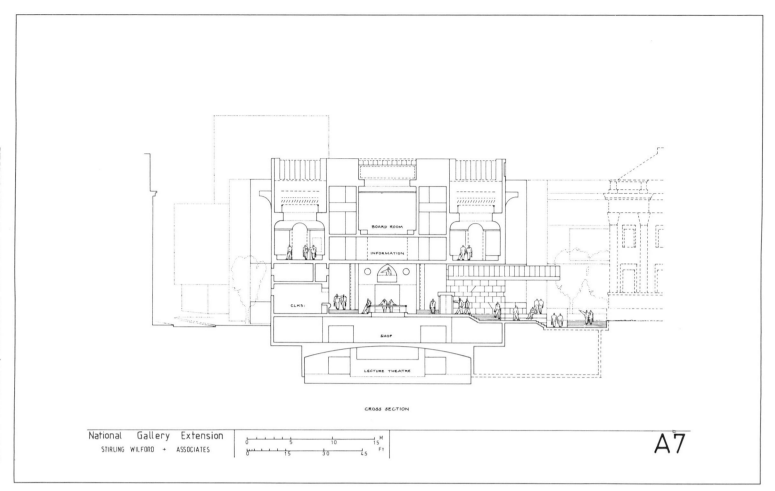

CROSS SECTION

National Gallery Extension
STIRLING WILFORD + ASSOCIATES

A7

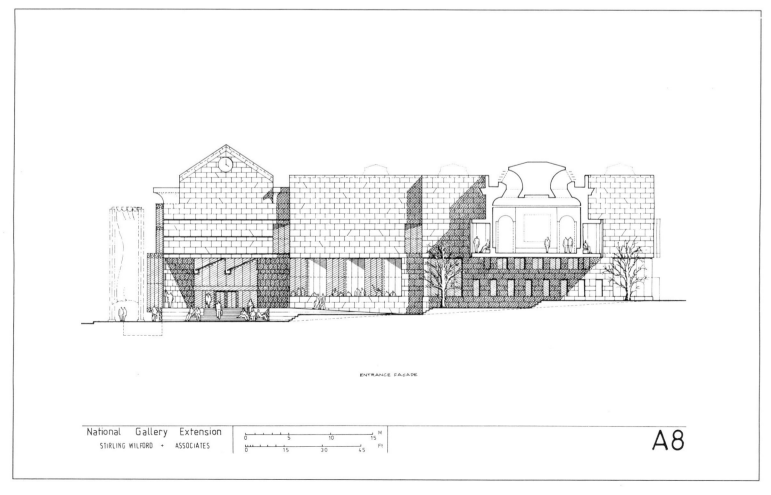

ENTRANCE FACADE

National Gallery Extension
STIRLING WILFORD + ASSOCIATES

A8

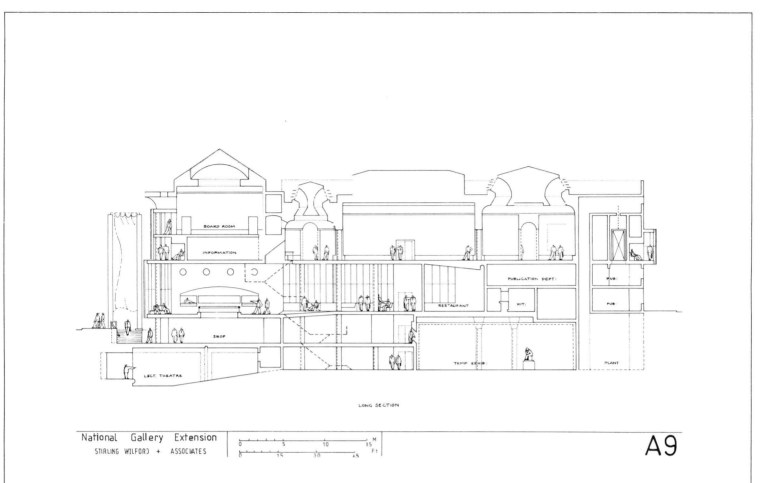

BOARD ROOM

INFORMATION

PUBLICATION DEPT:

PUB:

PUB:

SHOP

RESTAURANT

KIT:

LECT. THEATRE

TEMP. EXHIB:

PLANT

LONG SECTION

National Gallery Extension
STIRLING WILFORD + ASSOCIATES

A9

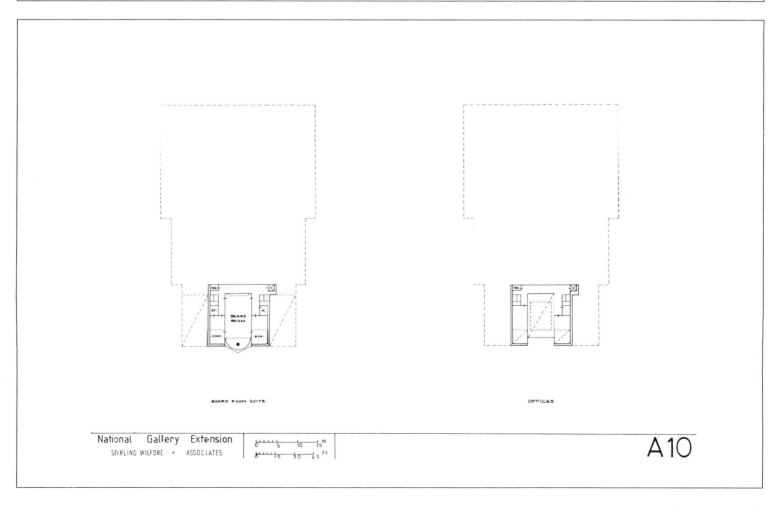

BOARD ROOM SUITE

OFFICES

National Gallery Extension
STIRLING WILFORD + ASSOCIATES

A10

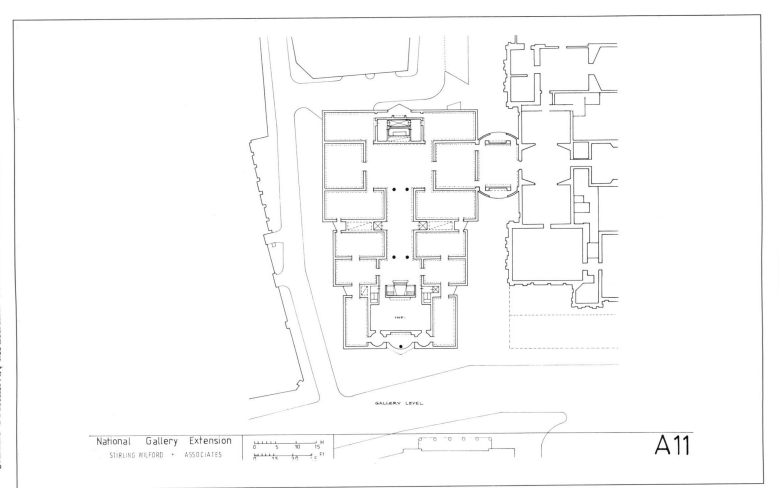

GALLERY LEVEL

National Gallery Extension

STIRLING WILFORD + ASSOCIATES

0    5    10    15    M
0    15    30    45    Ft

A11

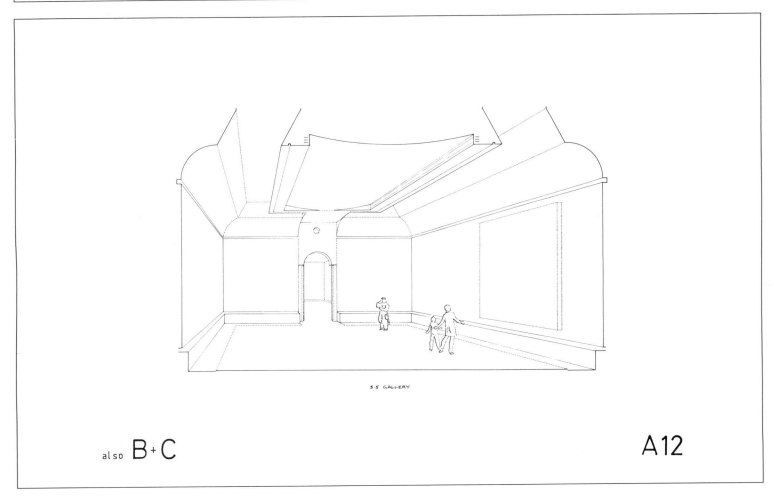

5·5 GALLERY

also B+C

A12

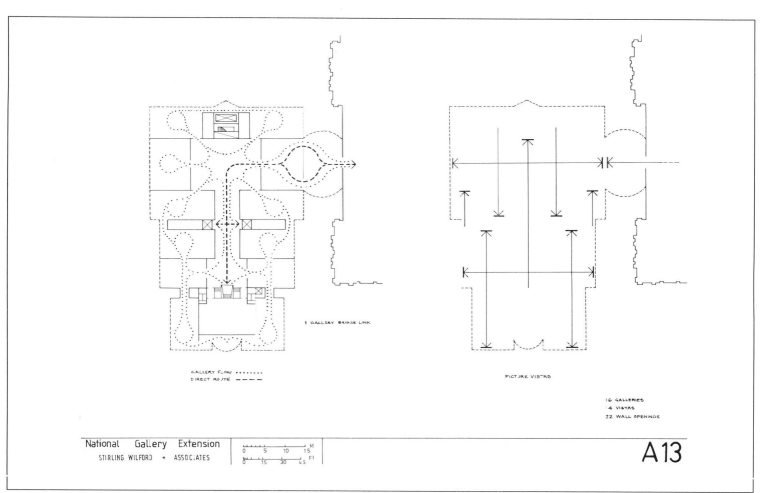

1 GALLERY BRIDGE LINK

GALLERY FLOW ·······
DIRECT ROUTE ─ ─ ─

PICTURE VISTAS

16 GALLERIES
4 VISTAS
32 WALL OPENINGS

National Gallery Extension
STIRLING WILFORD + ASSOCIATES

0  5  10  15 M
0  15  30  45 Ft

A13

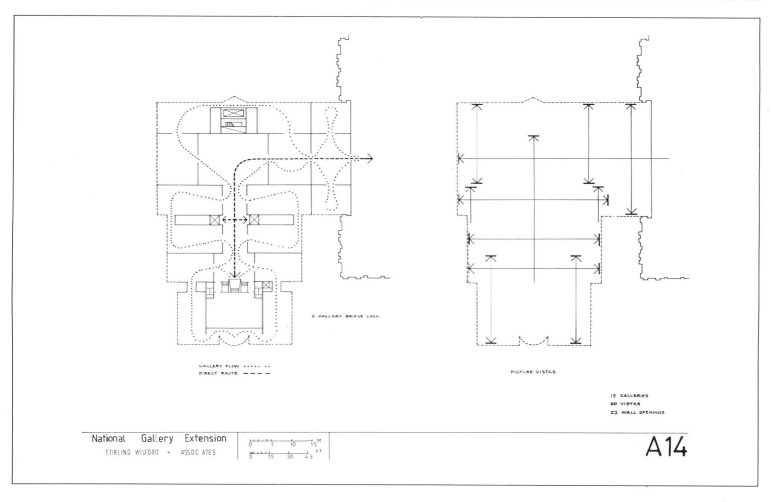

3 GALLERY BRIDGE LINK

GALLERY FLOW ······
DIRECT ROUTE ─ ─ ─

PICTURE VISTAS

13 GALLERIES
20 VISTAS
22 WALL OPENINGS

National Gallery Extension
STIRLING WILFORD + ASSOCIATES

0  5  10  15 M
0  15  30  45 Ft

A14

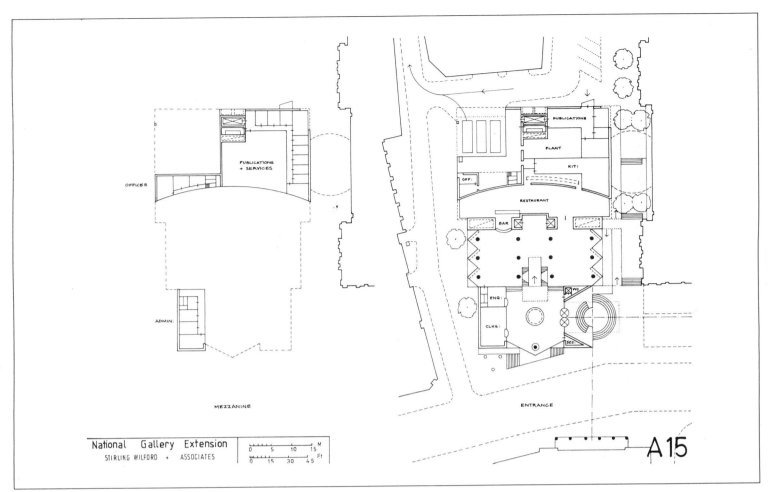

OFFICES

PUBLICATIONS + SERVICES

ADMIN:

MEZZANINE

PUBLICATIONS

PLANT

KIT:

OFF:

RESTAURANT

BAR

ENQ:

WC

CLKS:

SEC:

ENTRANCE

National Gallery Extension
STIRLING WILFORD + ASSOCIATES

A15

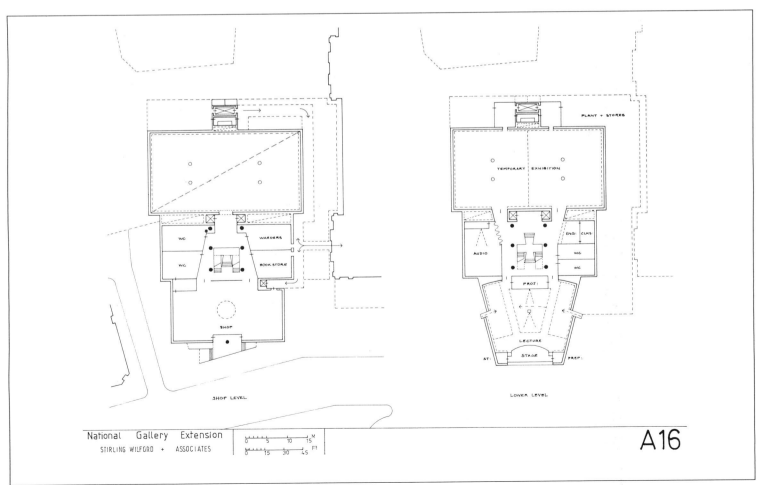

WC

WC

WARDERS

BOOK STORE

SHOP

SHOP LEVEL

PLANT + STORES

TEMPORARY EXHIBITION

AUDIO

ENQ: CLKS

WC

WC

PROJ:

LECTURE

ST:  STAGE  PREP:

LOWER LEVEL

National Gallery Extension
STIRLING WILFORD + ASSOCIATES

A16

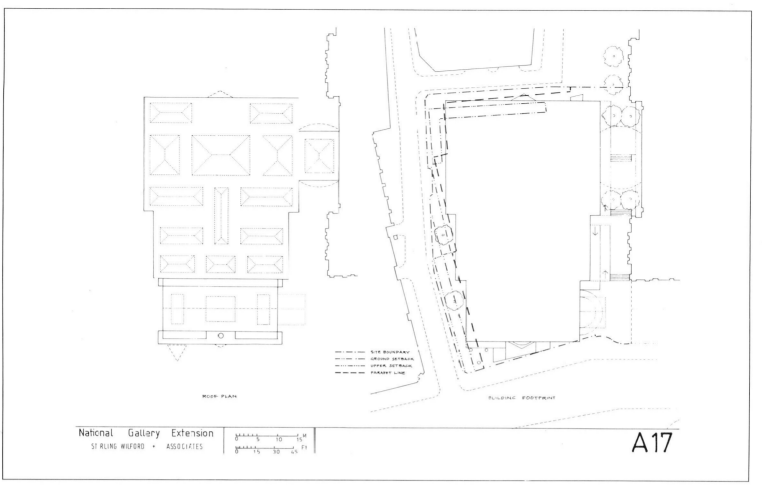

ROOF PLAN

BUILDING FOOTPRINT

--- · · · ·   SITE BOUNDARY
--- · --- · ·   GROUND SETBACK
--- --- --- ·   UPPER SETBACK
--- --- --- ---   PARAPET LINE

National Gallery Extension
STIRLING WILFORD · ASSOCIATES

0   5   10   15  M
0   15   30   45  Ft

A17

LIGHTING, AIR CONDITIONING AND STRUCTURE
Ove Arup and Partners

DAYLIGHTING (see details 1,5,).

Diffused natural light will be provided through reflective ceiling 'scoops' which is a development of the method tried and tested in other galleries by JSMWA. Shading by automatic external louvres above each scoop will prevent solar penetration and ensure 200 ± 50 lux over the picture wall. Illuminance will vary from 2½:1 in lower galleries to 3:1 in taller galleries. The louvres will be controlled by an internal sensor.

ARTIFICIAL LIGHTING (see details 1,2,5,6,7).

To provide a similarity of light source, the artificial lighting will be accommodated in the scoops. In the taller galleries flurescent luminaries with purpose-design reflectors will maximise direct light on the picture wall. To soften shadow lines from projecting picture frames, and to achieve proper illuminance at the bottom of the wall, a reflected component will be added to the direct lighting within the scoop. In the lower galleries, the artificial lighting will be indirect, being reflected off the sides of the scoop. Lamps will be selected for their colour rendering properties and be dimmer controlled.

Ultra-violet light will be eliminated from natural and artificial light by use of filters. Particular attention will be paid to achieve an energy efficient solution in what will be, by its nature, a low energy building.

AIR CONDITIONING (see details 1,4,8,9, 10).

The mechanical design fulfills the requirements of the 'Guidelines for Architects' and will meet the standards set out in the PSA Technical Report (M&E) TR70 in respect of air quality in gallery spaces. To achieve good circulation within the galleries, air will be supplied from high level and extracted at low level.

The planning allows for a simple service distribution pattern throughout the building. Plant at basement level is connected by three large vertical ducts to horizontal distribution in the roof above galleries. Plant for the upper galleries will comprise three 50% capacity units, including one standby. The temporary exhibition space will have separate plant and other areas such as the lecture theatre will be provided with air conditioning or ventilation as necessary. It is assumed that chilled water, heating water and electrical power will be provided from the energy centre in the existing building.

STRUCTURE

The project has been developed to minimise excavation and to make possible a simple and efficient structure. It comprises a reinforced concrete frame with a steel roof structure accommodating light scoops and maintenance access. Floors will be solid with downstand beam, or a troughed slab. The planning allows continuous columns to transfer load from the roof to foundations. The substructure includes piled raft foundations with either diaphragm retaining walls or concrete lined sheet piling. If required by the Gallery, a column free temporary exhibition space could be achieved by incorporating a transfer structure into the floors above.

also B·C

A18

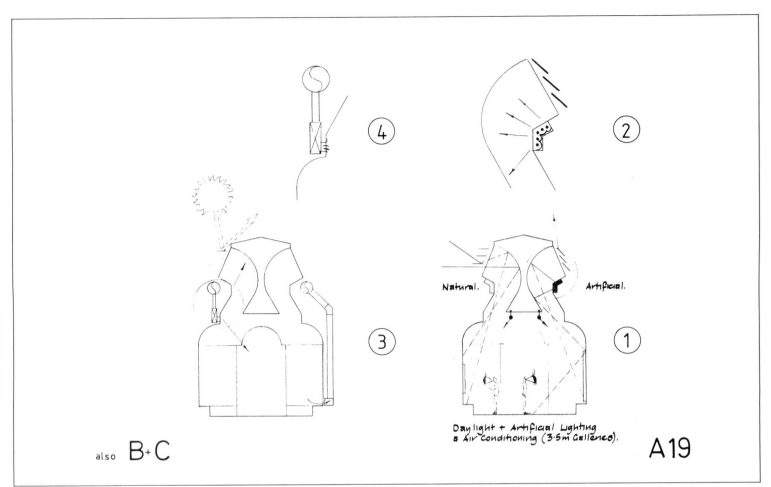

④

②

③

①

Natural.　Artificial.

Daylight + Artificial Lighting
& Air Conditioning (3·5m Galleries).

also B+C

A19

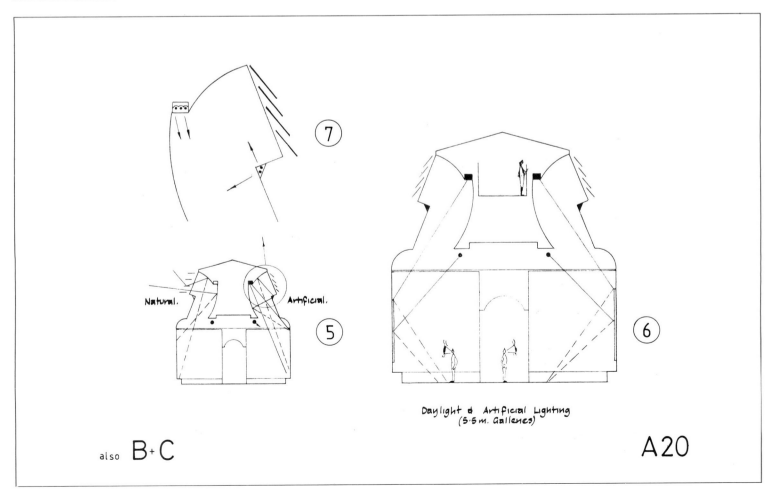

⑦

Natural.　Artificial.

⑤

⑥

Daylight & Artificial Lighting
(5·5m. Galleries)

also B+C

A20

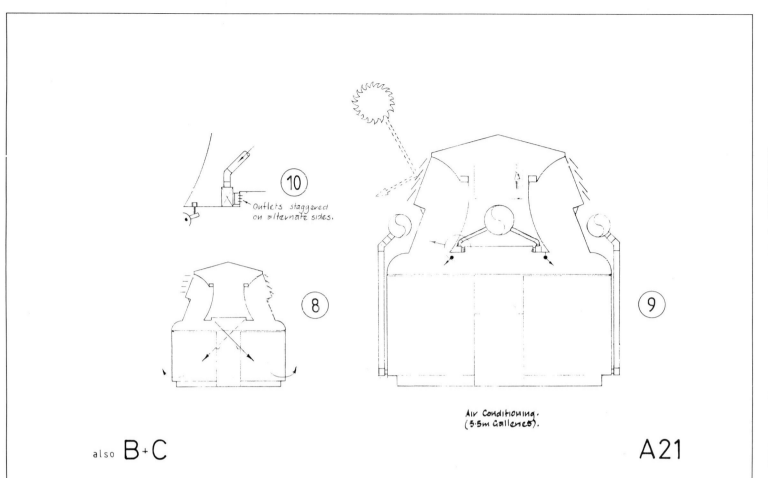

⑩ Outlets staggered on alternate sides.

⑧

also B+C

⑨

Air Conditioning.
(5·5m Galleries).

A21

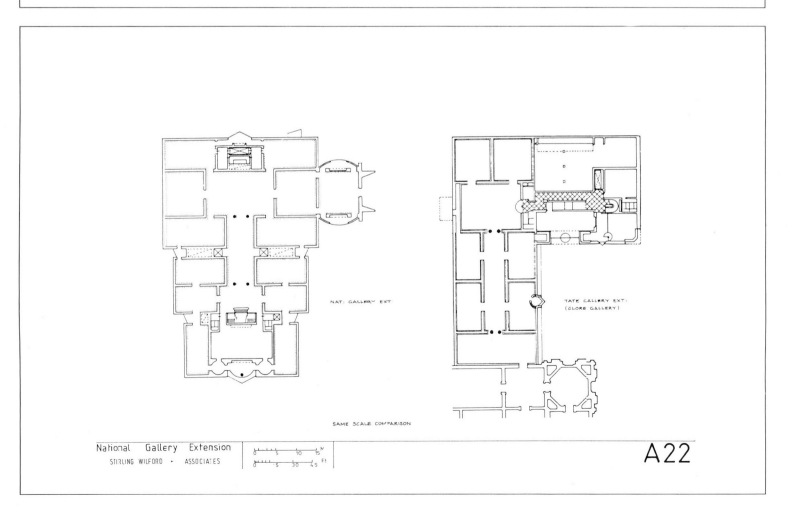

NAT: GALLERY EXT:

TATE GALLERY EXT:
(CLORE GALLERY)

SAME SCALE COMPARISON

National Gallery Extension
STIRLING WILFORD + ASSOCIATES

A22

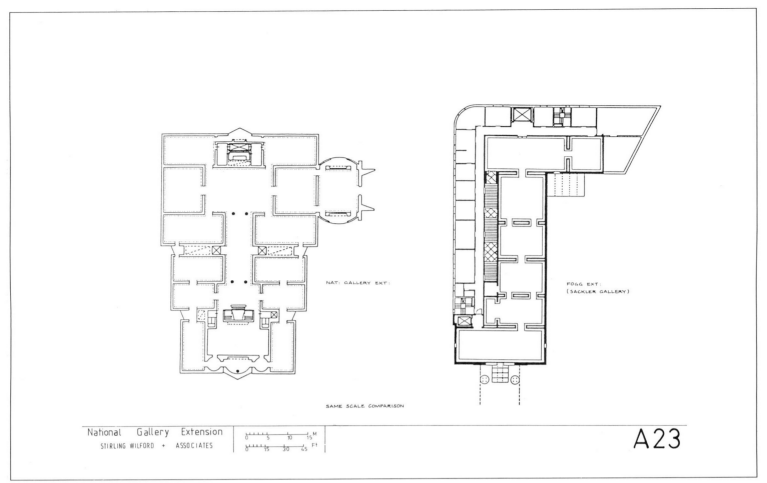

NAT: GALLERY EXT:

FOGG EXT:
(SACKLER GALLERY)

SAME SCALE COMPARISON

National Gallery Extension
STIRLING WILFORD + ASSOCIATES

A23

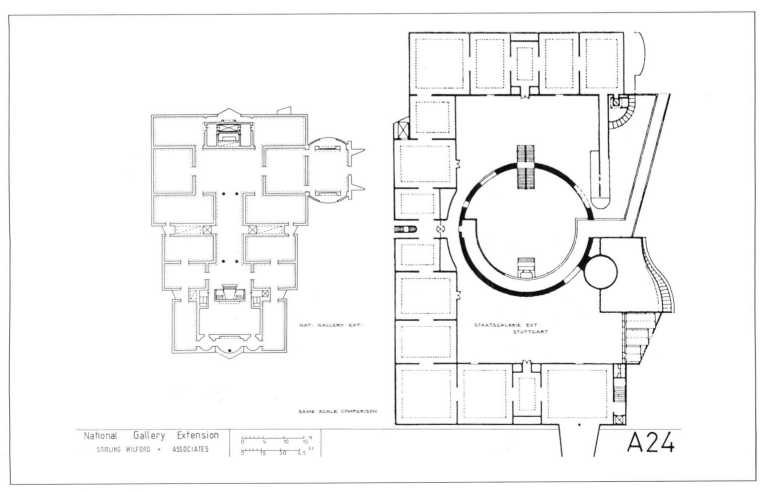

NAT: GALLERY EXT:

STAATSGALERIE EXT:
STUTTGART

SAME SCALE COMPARISON

National Gallery Extension
STIRLING WILFORD + ASSOCIATES

A24

SCHEME B
ACCOMMODATION

| | NATIONAL GALLERY GUIDELINES (m²) | AREAS ACHIEVED (m²) |
|---|---|---|
| 3.1 GALLERIES | 1320 plus<br>wall length - 400m plus | 1520 (15% increase) net<br>560m (40% increase) |
| 3.2 ENTRANCE VESTIBULE AND CLOAKROOM | 'spacious' | 478 |
| 3.3 LECTURE THEATRE | 400 seats | 400 seats |
| 3.4 PUBLICATIONS SHOP + STORE | 400 | 516 |
| 3.5 RESTAURANT | min 150 seats | 130 seats |
| 3.6 TEMPORARY EXHIBITION GALLERY + STORE | 700 - 1000 | 800 net |
| 3.7 AUDIO VISUAL | 100 - 150 seats | 130 seats |
| 3.8 INFORMATION ROOM | 150 | 130 |
| 3.9 MISC.<br>Warders Accommodation<br>Public Toilets<br>Service Entrance | 100<br>-<br>- | 116<br>140<br>260 |
| 3.11 PUBLICATIONS DEPARTMENT<br>Offices<br>Storage | 400<br>200 | 405<br>200 |
| 3.12 CAR PARKING | approx. 12 | 10 on St Martin's St. |

B1

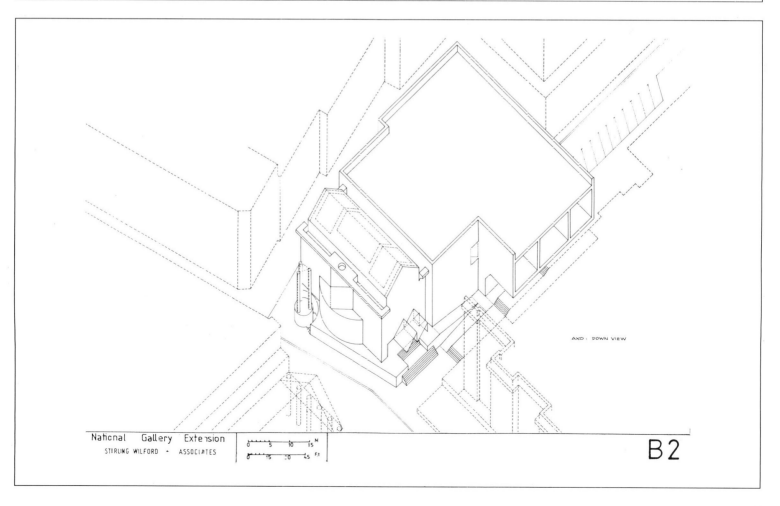

AXO : DOWN VIEW

National Gallery Extension
STIRLING WILFORD + ASSOCIATES

B2

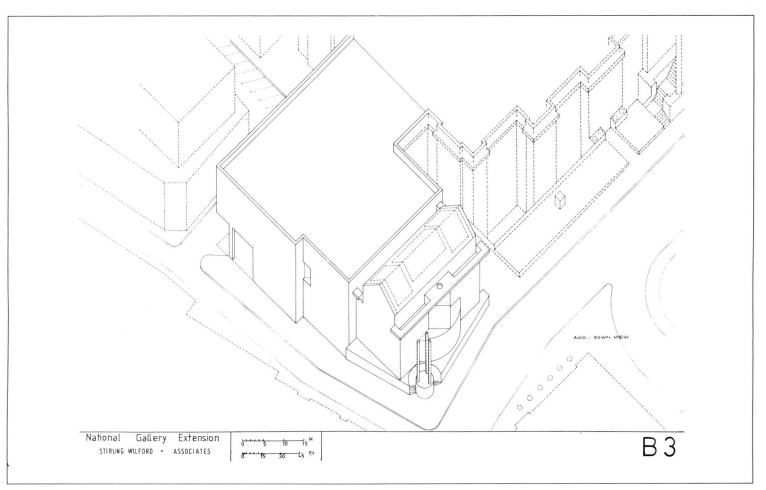

National Gallery Extension
STIRLING WILFORD + ASSOCIATES

AXO: DOWN VIEW

B 3

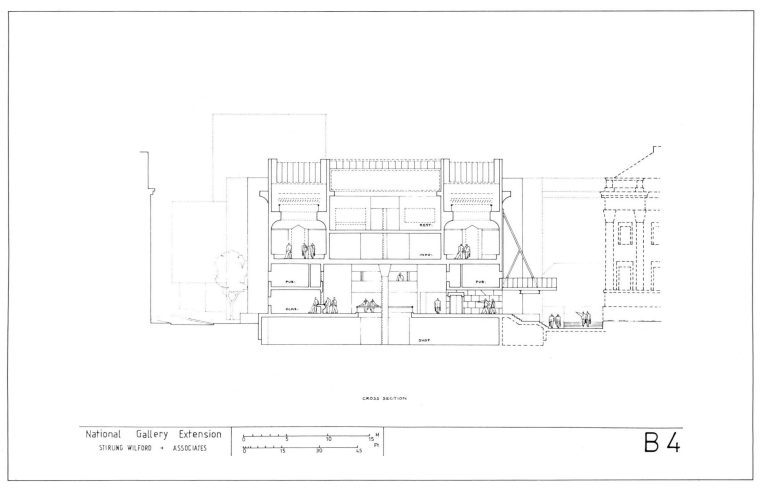

CROSS SECTION

National Gallery Extension
STIRLING WILFORD + ASSOCIATES

B 4

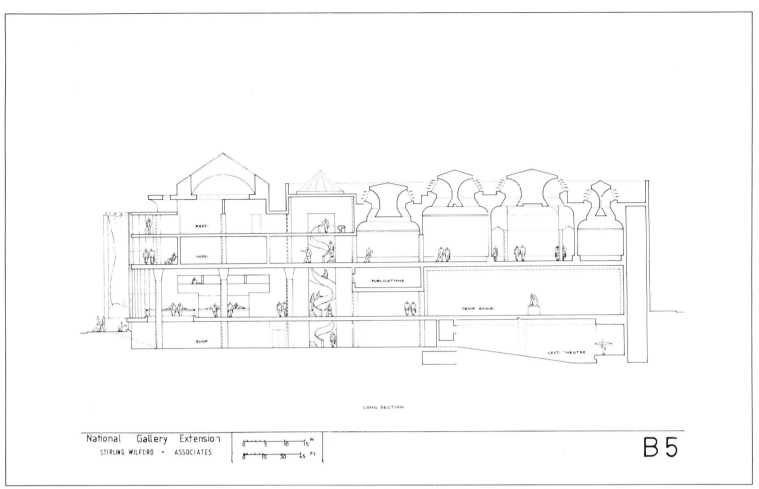

REST.

INFO.

PUBLICATIONS

SHOP

TEMP. EXHIB.

LECT. THEATRE

LONG SECTION

National Gallery Extension
STIRLING WILFORD + ASSOCIATES

0  5  10  15 M
0  15  30  45 Ft

B5

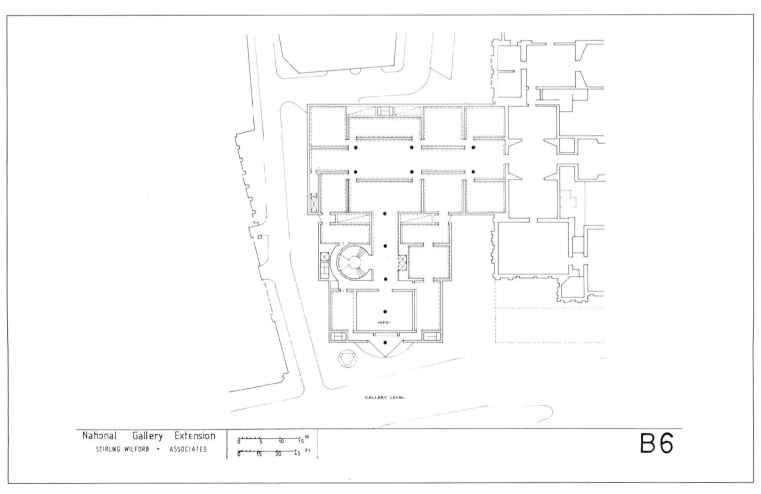

INFO.

GALLERY LEVEL

National Gallery Extension
STIRLING WILFORD + ASSOCIATES

0  5  10  15 M
0  15  30  45 Ft

B6

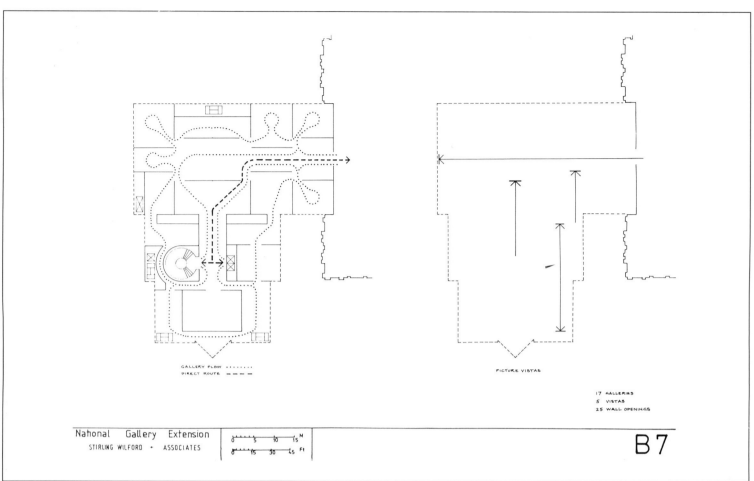

GALLERY FLOW .........
DIRECT ROUTE ━ ━ ━

PICTURE VISTAS

17 GALLERIES
5 VISTAS
25 WALL OPENINGS

National Gallery Extension
STIRLING WILFORD + ASSOCIATES

0 5 10 15 M
0 15 30 45 Ft

B 7

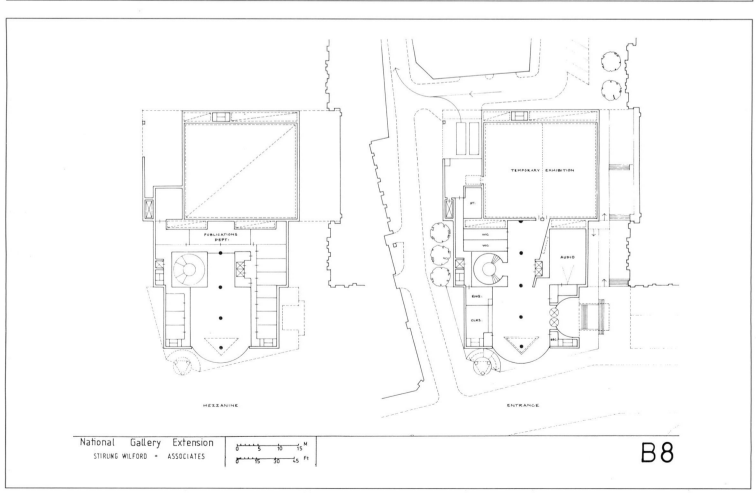

MEZZANINE

ENTRANCE

National Gallery Extension
STIRLING WILFORD + ASSOCIATES

0 5 10 15 M
0 15 30 45 Ft

B 8

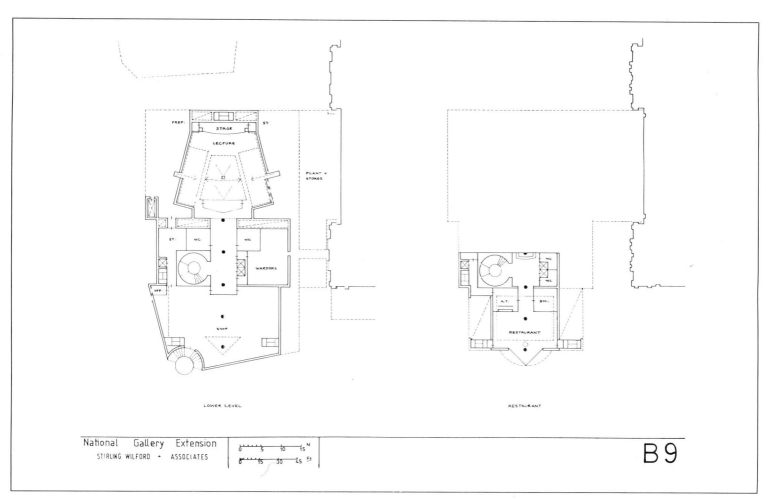

LOWER LEVEL                                    RESTAURANT

National   Gallery   Extension     0  5   10   15 M
STIRLING  WILFORD  +  ASSOCIATES   0  15   30   45 Ft

**B 9**

|  |  | NATIONAL GALLERY GUIDELINES (m$^2$) | SCHEME C ACCOMMODATION AREAS ACHIEVED (m$^2$) |
|---|---|---|---|
| 3.1 | GALLERIES | 1320 plus<br>wall length – 400m plus | 1552 (17.5% increase) net<br>568m (42% increase) |
| 3.2 | ENTRANCE VESTIBULE AND CLOAKROOM | 'spacious' | 638 |
| 3.3 | LECTURE THEATRE | 400 seats | 400 seats |
| 3.4 | PUBLICATIONS SHOP + STORE | 400 | 500 |
| 3.5 | RESTAURANT | min 150 seats | 230 seats |
| 3.6 | TEMPORARY EXHIBITION GALLERY + STORE | 700 – 1000 | 902 net |
| 3.7 | AUDIO VISUAL | 100 – 150 seats | 120 seats |
| 3.8 | INFORMATION ROOM | 150 | 162 |
| 3.9 | MISC.<br>Warders Accommodation<br>Public Toilets<br>Service Entrance | 100<br>–<br>– | 90<br>150<br>230 |
| 3.12 | CAR PARKING | approx. 12 | 10 on St Martin's Street |

**C1**

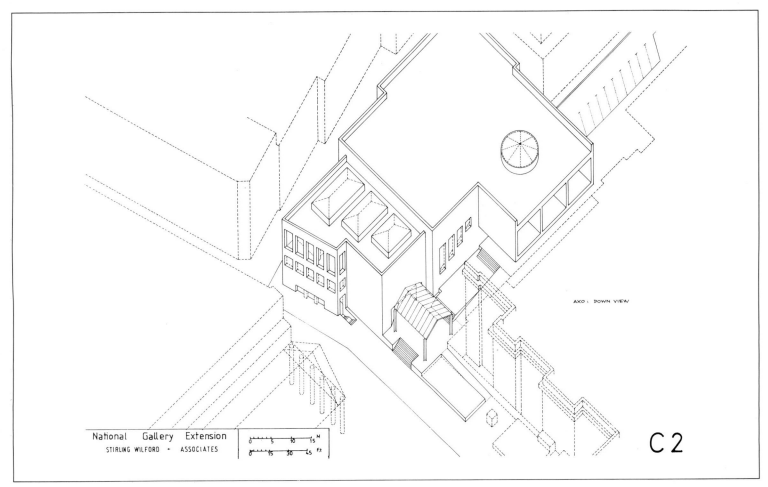

National Gallery Extension
STIRLING WILFORD + ASSOCIATES

AXO: DOWN VIEW

C 2

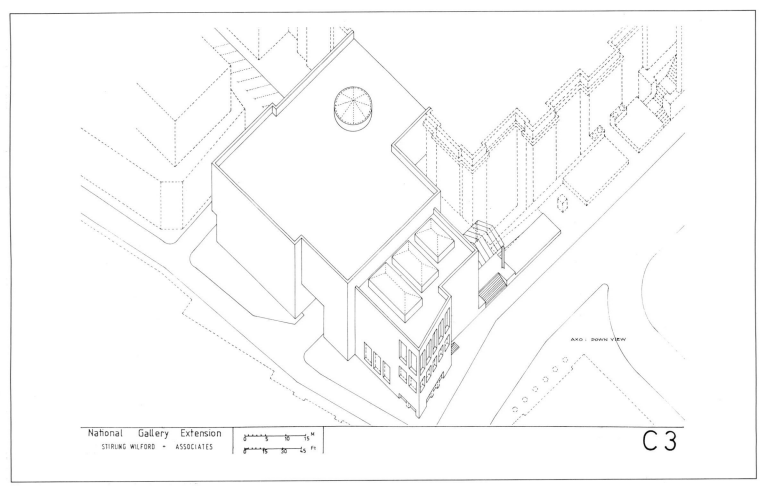

National Gallery Extension
STIRLING WILFORD + ASSOCIATES

AXO: DOWN VIEW

C 3

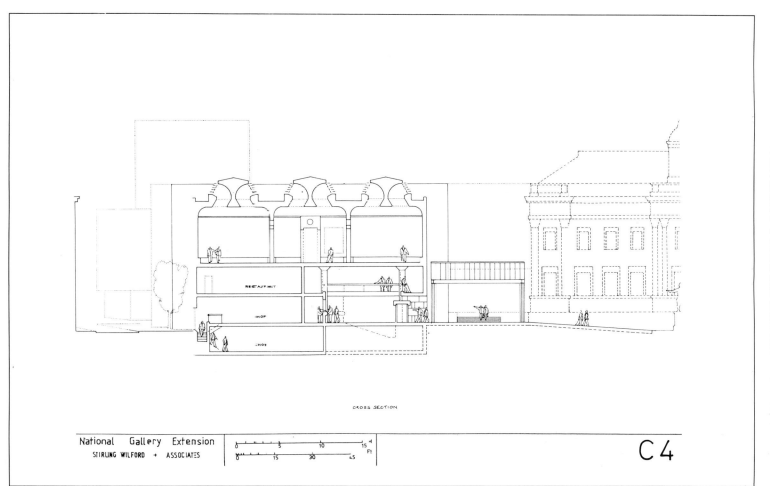

CROSS SECTION

National Gallery Extension

STIRLING WILFORD + ASSOCIATES

C 4

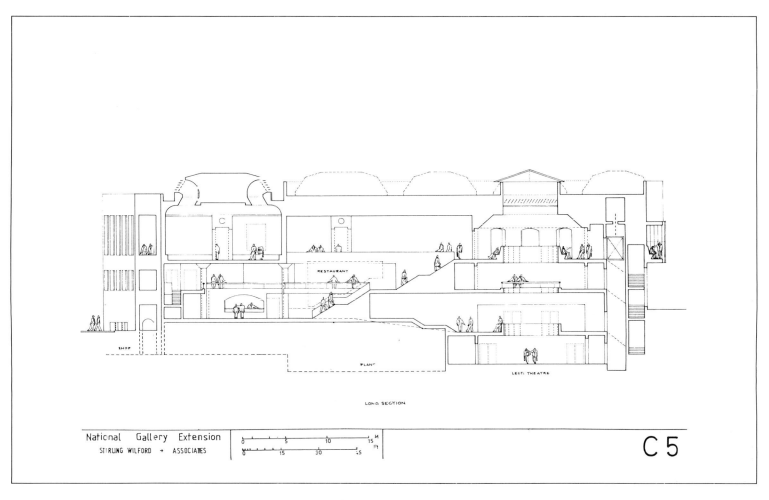

RESTAURANT

SHOP

PLAN

LECT: THEATRE

LONG SECTION

National Gallery Extension

STIRLING WILFORD + ASSOCIATES

C 5

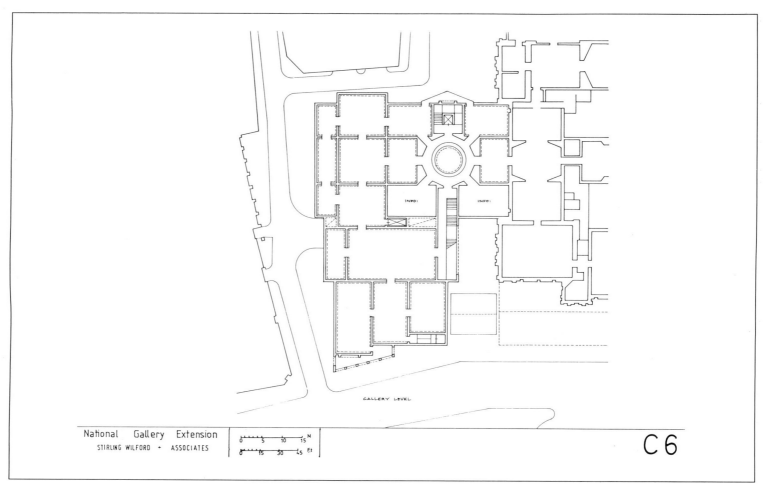

GALLERY LEVEL

National Gallery Extension
STIRLING WILFORD + ASSOCIATES

0 5 10 15 M
0 15 30 45 Ft

C 6

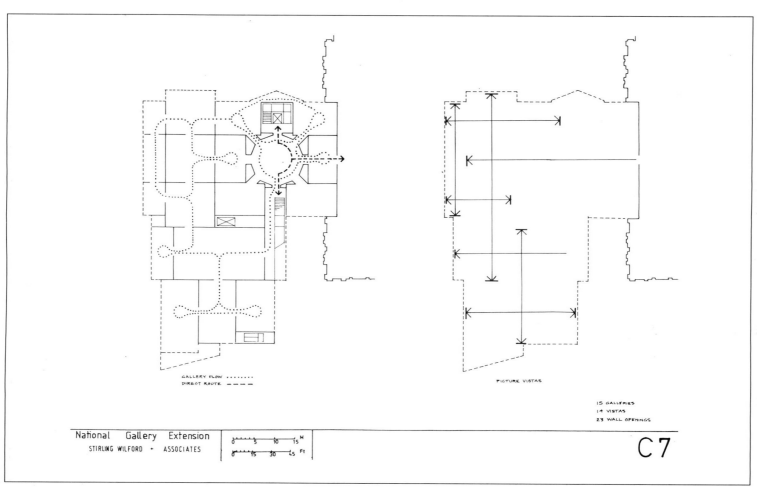

GALLERY FLOW ........
DIRECT ROUTE — — — —

PICTURE VISTAS

15 GALLERIES
14 VISTAS
23 WALL OPENINGS

National Gallery Extension
STIRLING WILFORD + ASSOCIATES

0 5 10 15 M
0 15 30 45 Ft

C 7

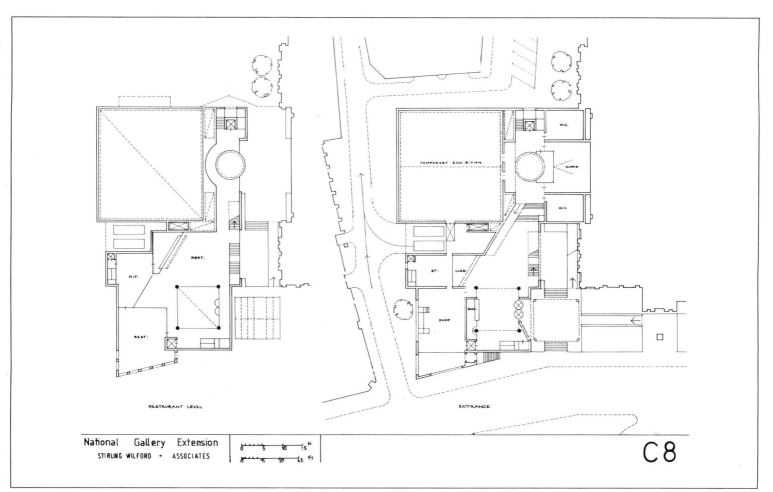

RESTAURANT LEVEL

ENTRANCE

National Gallery Extension
STIRLING WILFORD + ASSOCIATES

C8

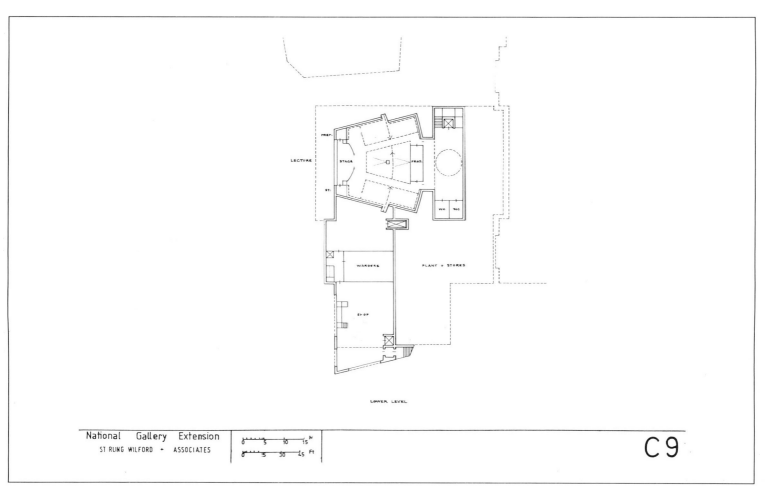

LOWER LEVEL

National Gallery Extension
STIRLING WILFORD + ASSOCIATES

C9

<u>PRELIMINARY PROGRAMME</u>

<u>DESIGN (PRE CONSTRUCTION)</u>

DEVELOPMENT OF COMPREHENSIVE BRIEF WITH CLIENT AND SUBMIT OUTLINE PLANNING     3 - 4 MONTHS

DESIGN DEVELOPMENT ( SCHEME DESIGN ) AND SUBMIT DETAIL PLANNING     5 - 6 MONTHS *

FULLY DETAILED PRODUCTION DRAWINGS AND SPECIFICATIONS     12 MONTHS #

                         TOTAL   <u>20 - 22 MONTHS</u>

<u>CONSTRUCTION</u>

STRUCTURE BELOW GROUND     9 MONTHS

SUPERSTRUCTURE AND ROOF WATERTIGHTNESS     11 MONTHS

FINISHES ( inc 4 - 5 months service operation )     11 MONTHS

                         TOTAL     <u>31 MONTHS</u>

\*   Assumes no public enquiry
\#   Sequential tendering system (MC or CM) might reduce this stage by 36 - 40%

note: It is proposed that an early contract is let for civil engineering works including diaphragm walls, excavation piling and ground slab. This could begin six months before completion of the design stage, effectively reducing the construction period after design completion to two years one month.

---

<u>PRELIMINARY COST ESTIMATE</u>
Davis Belfield and Everest

| ELEMENT | | SCHEME | <u>A</u> ($8680m^2$) | SCHEME | <u>B</u> ($8120m^2$) | SCHEME | <u>C</u> ($8560m^2$) |
|---|---|---|---|---|---|---|---|
| | | $£/m^2$ | £ | $£/m^2$ | £ | $£/m^2$ | £ |
| Structure, envelope, internal walls and partitions | | 771 | 6,690,000 | 736 | 5,980,000 | 738 | 6,320,000 |
| Internal finishes, fittings and loose furniture | | 525 | 4,560,000 | 514 | 4,170,000 | 520 | 4,450,000 |
| Services installations and builder's work in connection | | 625 | 5,430,000 | 626 | 5,080,000 | 627 | 5,370,000 |
| External works | | 75 | 650,000 | 80 | 650,000 | 76 | 650,000 |
| | | 1,996 | 17,330,000 | 1,956 | 15,880,000 | 1,961 | 16,790,000. |
| Pre-construction design development allowance | 7.5% | 150 | 1,305,000 | 147 | 1,195,000 | 147 | 1,260,000 |
| Construction contingency | 2.5% | 54 | 465,000 | 52 | 425,000 | 53 | 450,000 |
| <u>TOTAL</u> | | 2,200 | 19,100,000 | 2,155 | 17,500,000 | 2,161 | 18,500,000. |

The above figures, which are at current price levels, include preliminaries, professional fees and fitting out but exclude VAT.

COMPARATIVE ACCOMMODATION SCHEDULE

| | GUIDELINES (m²) | AREAS ACHIEVED (m²) A | B | C |
|---|---|---|---|---|
| 3.1 GALLERIES | 1320 plus<br>400m plus wall length | 1640 (+24%) net<br>585m (+46%) | 1520 (-15%) net<br>560m (-40%) | 1552 (+17.5%) net<br>568m (+42%) |
| 3.2 ENTRANCE VESTIBULE AND CLOAKROOM | 'spacious' | 710 | 478 | 638 |
| 3.3 LECTURE THEATRE | 400 seats | 400 seats | 400 seats | 400 seats |
| 3.4 PUBLICATIONS SHOP + STORE | 400 | 465 | 516 | 500 |
| 3.5 RESTAURANT | min 150 seats | 185 seats | 130 seats | 230 seats |
| 3.6 TEMPORARY EXHIBITION GALLERY + STORE | 700 - 1000 | 1010 net | 800 net | 902 net |
| 3.7 AUDIO VISUAL | 100 - 150 seats | 125 seats | 130 seats | 120 seats |
| 3.8 INFORMATION ROOM | 150 | 120 | 130 | 162 |
| 3.9 MISC. | | | | |
|   Warders Accommodation | 100 | 100 | 116 | 90 |
|   Public Toilets | - | 135 | 140 | 150 |
|   Service Entrance | - | 420 (3 trucks) | 260 | 230 |
| | | | | |
| 3.10 BOARDROOM, DINING AND COMMITTEE ROOM | 200 | 220 | - | - |
| 3.11 PUBLICATIONS DEPARTMENT | | | | |
|   Offices | 400 | 550 | 405 | - |
|   Storage | 200 | 200 | 200 | - |
| 3.12 CAR PARKING | approx. 12 | 10 on<br>St Martin's St. | 10 on<br>St Martin's St. | 10 on<br>St Martin's St. |
| | | | | |
| ACCOMMODATION ALSO PROVIDED: | | | | |
| a) Cloakroom and Tickets for Temporary Exhibition | - | 50 | - | - |
| b) Administration and Services Offices | - | 165 | - | - |

JAMES STIRLING, MICHAEL WILFORD & ASSOCIATES

This report is published page for page but slightly reduced from the original A4 in full and unabridged form at the request of James Stirling Michael Wilford and Associates.

# AD Architectural Design

**ARCHITECTURAL DESIGN** is internationally recognised as being foremost among a small number of publications providing up-to-date information on architecture of the present and past. Each issue presents an in-depth analysis of a theme of relevance to architectural practice today, whether it be the work of an important new architect, a currently influential figure or movement, or the emergence of a new style or consensus of opinion. The high standard of writing, editorial selection and presentation has made *Architectural Design* one of the world's most progressive architectural magazines and essential reading for anyone interested in the art of architecture.

Themes covered recently by *Architectural Design* include the polemical work and projects of **Leon Krier**, the theoretical writings and teaching of the Russian Constructivist **Iakov Chernikhov**, the **UIA Exhibition** in Cairo, cross-currents of **American Architecture** and the collection of architectural works in the recently opened **German Architecture Museum**. Forthcoming issues include the **Vienna: Dream and Reality** Exhibition coordinated by Hans Hollein, **Tradition: Convention and Invention** by Lucien Steil, and **Designing A House** by Charles Jencks and Terry Farrell.

**ART & DESIGN** is already acknowledged as the best and only new monthly magazine covering the whole spectrum of the arts. Each issue contains editorial features on the latest developments in art, architecture, design, fashion, music and photography, together with a roundup of news covering products, books, salerooms, gossip, record reviews and extensive listings of both public and private galleries.

In addition to the high quality of editorial features by well-known contributors who are experts in their field, the current issues each contain a free original lithograph by a notable contemporary artist. *Art & Design* is available nationally from newsstands each month, or to make sure you get your copy you can take out a joint subscription to *Art & Design* and *Architectural Design* by completing the subscription form below.

A subscription will give you annually six double issues of *Architectural Design* and ten issues of *Art & Design* at a saving of over £20 or $40 on their value if purchased individually. To take advantage of this value-for-money offer, and to ensure that you get your copy regularly, fill in the form below and return it today:

---